REWIRED LEADERSHIP

Rewired Leadership: What Experts Have to Say

"If you're a leader, talent strategist, or HR executive staring down the barrel of the AI revolution, *Rewired Leadership*™ is the wake-up call you didn't know you needed. Mark Zides doesn't just talk about change, he demands it, and he's got the playbook to back it up. This *is not* just another leadership book. It *is* a blueprint for surviving and thriving in the agentic AI era. Zides combines sharp diagnosis with actionable solutions, and he's not afraid to call out the uncomfortable truths. If you're ready to trade control for clarity, heroics for systems, and comfort for relevance, this book will show you how. If you're not, well . . . you might want to start unlearning that, too."

—Rob Lauber, Former CLO of McDonalds

"Mark Zides' ability to stay one step ahead of emerging trends and shifting markets has been a defining hallmark of his career. *Rewired Leadership* reflects that same foresight—cutting through the AI hype to focus on what truly differentiates winners: sharper thinking, deeper listening, and disciplined, human-centered leadership all while moving at warp speed. Mark brings rare credibility from decades in boardrooms and high-growth environments, pairing practical frameworks with hard-earned judgment and humility. This book isn't just timely—it's a clear, grounded guide for leaders who want to turn AI into an advantage without losing their edge or their values."

—Jim Coghlin, Vice Chairman & Chief Supply Chain Officer, Coghlin Companies., Inc.

"AI has changed the rules of leadership. The legacy model—command-and-control and gut feel—won't cut it. *Rewired Leadership* replaces it with measurable behaviors, data-driven cadence, and human-centered judgment. As a friend and colleague of Mark Zides, I've watched this framework begin to elevate teams and outcomes in real time. It's a must read."

—John Lentine, Chief Revenue Officer, commercetools

When AI Changes Everything...

REWIRED
LEADERSHIP

...Unlearn Faster. Build Trust. Drive Impact.

MARK ZIDES

REWIRED LEADERSHIP
By Mark Zides

ISBN: 979-8-9941168-3-8
Ebook ISBN: 979-8-9941168-2-1
Library of Congress Control Number: *Pending*
For permission requests, email the publisher at:
Of The Day Press
ofthedaypress@gmail.com

Of The Day Press
Broomfield, Colorado

Printed in the United States of America
10 9 8 7 6 5 4 3 2 1
First Edition

Contents

Chapter 4

Chapter 5

Chapter 6

Chapter 7

Chapter 8

Chapter 9

Chapter 10

Chapter 11

Chapter 12

Chapter 17

Chapter 18

Chapter 19

Conclusion

Appendix

Foreword

By Michael Glass
Global Talent Leader

A FEW MONTHS AGO, ON A FLIGHT FROM SAN Diego to Boston, I sat next to the CFO of a global manufacturing company. He was buried in his laptop, surrounded by dashboards and predictive models. After a while, he sighed and said, "We have more data than I ever imagined-and somehow, I understand my people less."

That line stuck with me. It captures what so many leaders are feeling right now.

Artificial intelligence has given us visibility into everything, except the one thing that's hardest to measure: leadership itself.

That's why Mark Zides wrote *Rewired Leadership*.

If you know Mark, you know he's allergic to buzzwords and pretense. He's not here to sell a new management trick or to make anyone sound like a futurist. His focus is simpler and harder. He wants us to be better at being human in a world that's getting smarter by the minute. His belief is that AI isn't a technology problem but a leadership problem. It's a challenge to every one of us leading through uncertainty.

This book offers practical ways to reset how we lead, not by moving faster or shouting louder, but by pausing, paying attention, and listening before deciding.

He'll push you to:

- Use AI as a tool that sharpens your thinking, not one that replaces it.
- Treat curiosity as a practice, not a passing mood.
- Trade control for trust and confusion for honest conversation.
- Remember that good judgment matters more than clever systems.

Mark's perspective comes from experience—three decades of building, fixing, and leading teams in companies large and small. He's seen what works when the pressure is high and the future unclear. Leadership, in his view, isn't a title or a strategy deck; it's a daily commitment to clarity, courage, and care.

Technology will keep speeding up. The demands on leaders will only grow. It's tempting to hand decisions to algorithms and hope they get it right. But leadership has never been about perfection. It's about presence—showing up, listening, deciding, and doing it again tomorrow.

That's what *Rewired Leadership* helps leaders do. Mark offers a grounded framework for thinking straight when the world around you moves fast. He shows how to stay curious, make decisions you're proud of, and keep your team focused when everything else feels like noise.

The leaders who will thrive in this new era aren't the ones chasing every new tool. They're the ones who can stay calm, make sense of complexity, and help their teams do the same. That's what this book is about and why it couldn't have come at a better time.

—Michael Glass, Head of Talent Management and Learning & Development at ResMed

Introduction

LEADERSHIP IS BEING REDEFINED RIGHT IN front of us. Markets shift in real time. Technology evolves faster than most organizations can understand. Customers expect immediate relevance. Employees expect meaning, development, and trust. And every quarter feels more compressed than the one before. The future of leadership is no longer about who has the most experience. It is about who can unlearn the fastest.

Yet many leaders continue operating with reflexes built for a slower world. They rely on decision habits that were effective ten years ago but now create drag. They cling to the feeling that experience should matter more than adaptability. They expect teams to work differently, but they lead the same way they always have. They push for innovation while protecting routines that flatten creativity. They want speed but unintentionally slow everything down.

None of this is a character flaw. It is a wiring issue. Years of success built strong habits, but those habits were built for a different era. You cannot lead today with yesterday's assumptions. And you cannot expect transformation from your teams if you are not transforming yourself.

I've seen this pattern for three decades, and now, with agentic AI—artificial intelligence that can act with a degree of autonomy to achieve goals—on the rise, the clock is ticking faster than ever. The leaders who refuse to unlearn aren't just creating drag; they're signing their own irrelevance mandate. If you are not actively rewiring your mindset and your operating system, you are falling behind. Period.

The gap between what organizations need and how leaders show up is widening. High performers crave challenge and growth. New talent wants purpose and transparency. Teams want clarity and empowerment. Organizations want experimentation, speed, and resilience. Customers want personalization and immediacy. These demands all converge on one singular truth: Leaders must unlearn the habits that block speed, fog clarity, and crush humanity.

This book is your playbook.

Chapter 1

The Leadership Rewire—Why Expertise Is Now Your Enemy

LEADERSHIP HAS ALWAYS BEEN SHAPED BY ONE defining factor: *how work gets done.* When work moves slowly, leadership can be deliberate. When work is predictable, leadership can rely on experience. When information flows upward and decisions flow downward, leadership naturally becomes hierarchical.

For most of modern business history, this model worked. Leaders planned. Teams executed. Managers coordinated. Decisions were escalated, reviewed, approved, and communicated back down the chain. Time acted as a buffer. Mistakes could be caught. Alignment could be built through meetings.

But leadership was never timeless. It was contextual. And that context has now fundamentally changed.

Today, work no longer moves in sequence. It moves continuously. Signals surface in real time. Decisions are not discrete events—they are ongoing flows. Automation handles routine tasks. AI surfaces insights instantly. Teams operate across time zones, platforms, and systems.

Leadership that was designed to *manage* work is now being asked to *enable* work. That shift is what this book calls the *leadership rewire.*

WHY THE OLD MODEL IS BREAKING

Most leaders are doing exactly what they were trained to do. They stay close to the work. They attend more meetings. They insert themselves where things slow down. They make decisions when others hesitate. Individually, these behaviors feel responsible. Collectively, they create *drag*.

The single biggest roadblock to your future success is not a lack of new ideas it's your devotion to old ones. The harder leaders try to control speed, the more they slow it down. This is not because leaders lack capability or commitment. It is because the environment has changed faster than leadership habits. You are the victim of your own success. *Your expertise is now your enemy.*

This is not incompetence. It's not malice. It's *unlearning debt*—the dangerous accumulation of outdated assumptions, reflexes, and beliefs that were once a strength but are now a massive, invisible drag on your organization. Every leader, at some point, enters the *unlearning curve*—the period where their accumulated expertise begins to generate negative returns.

Stage of the Unlearning Curve	Leader Behavior	Impact on Organizational Speed
The Expert's Plateau	Reliance on past methods; resistance to changing internal processes.	**Slow Decision-Making:** "We've always done it this way" culture; innovation requires endless validation.
The Control Fallacy	Micromanaging the "how"; fear of delegating autonomy in new areas (like agentic AI strategy).	**Talent Attrition & Bottlenecking:** High performers leave; the leader is the chief bottleneck, crushing team burnout.
The Relevance Cliff	Failure to integrate new technology or adopt new market narratives.	**Organizational Obsolescence:** Market lag; competitive disadvantage; failure to pivot to the Agentic Economy.

THE CORE MESSAGE OF REWIRED LEADERSHIP™

The leaders who thrive in the AI age are the ones who can unlearn faster than the world changes rewiring their mindset, habits, and operating system to unlock human performance at a pace technology alone can never achieve.

In the age of AI, leadership isn't about knowing more—it's about unlearning faster.

This book is about transforming your leadership from a legacy operating system built on control and experience, to a *Rewired Leadership*™ operating system built on clarity, speed, and adaptive intelligence. It is the definitive guide for chief executive officers (CEOs), chief human resource officers (CHROs), and every leader who understands that the only way to master the future is to unlearn the past.

THE REWIRED CEO: LEADING AT THE INTERSECTION OF AI, PEOPLE, AND PERFORMANCE

The role of the CEO is being structurally redesigned. It is no longer enough to be a great allocator of capital; you must be a great allocator of *attention* and *organizational energy.* Where previous CEOs focused on managing structure and resources, the *Rewired* CEO must manage the *speed of adaptation* and the *quality of human insight.*

The new reality is that the biggest drag on growth is no longer the market or the competition—it's organizational friction. Legacy leadership habits—slow decision loops, unnecessary layers of approval, and a culture of risk-aversion are the silent killers of enterprise value. The *Rewired* CEO recognizes that their primary job is to eliminate this friction and establish a high-performance operating system that is fundamentally human-centered, yet AI-enabled.

The Rewired CEO Mindset Shifts

Legacy CEO Mindset	Rewired CEO Mindset (The Unlearning)
Control: Must know every detail and sign off on all major decisions.	**Intent:** Defines the mission and the non-negotiables, then grants radical autonomy for the *how*.
Experience: Believes past success dictates future strategy.	**Adaptability:** Believes the rate of unlearning dictates future survival.
Complexity: Tolerates bureaucracy and complicated reporting lines.	**Clarity & Speed:** Ruthlessly eliminates complexity to reduce the time between insight and execution.
Talent as Cost: Focuses on efficiency and headcount reduction.	**Talent as IP:** Focuses on human capability building and maximizing adaptive intelligence.

The first step in *Rewired Leadership*™ at the top is to unlearn the need for control. You must pivot from being the chief *problem-solver* to the chief *system architect*. Your job is to build the environment where the best ideas can surface, where talent is motivated by mission, and where the culture moves at the speed of the market. This requires a profound personal unlearning of the very habits that earned you the corner office.

AI WILL NOT REPLACE LEADERS— IT WILL EXPOSE THEM

Here is the blunt truth no one wants to say in the boardroom: AI is not primarily an economic threat; it is a *leadership spotlight*. AI is quietly (and in some cases, not so quietly) rewriting the rules of leadership. Not by competing with executives on spreadsheets or strategy decks, but by changing what organizations actually need from the people in charge. It will not replace you, but it will expose every single outdated, lazy, or ineffective leadership habit you possess. And it will expose them *fast.*

The exposure is not about firing leaders; it is about rendering their current behaviors strategically redundant. Consider the middle manager whose primary function is translating executive intent into daily tasks and reporting progress up the chain. AI can now handle the translation (via agentic planning) and the reporting (via real-time dashboards). The leader's involvement becomes pure friction—a human bottleneck in an automated loop.

This necessitates a profound unlearning: The highest value leader is not the one who knows the most, but the one who can enable the organization to move with the most speed and clarity.

THE EXPOSURE THESIS: WHY YOUR VALUE PROPOSITION IS SHRINKING

Research from firms like McKinsey & Company confirms that the value of human labor is rapidly migrating away from predictable, data-intensive, and procedural tasks. This means the individual leader's value proposition is shrinking if it relies on:

- **Information Synthesis:** Organizing and interpreting large data sets.
- **Routine Coordination:** Managing linear process flows and ensuring compliance.
- **Historical Precedent:** Relying on "how we did it last time" to guide future action.

These are precisely the functions that agentic AI handles flawlessly, tirelessly, and instantly. Your job is now to master the messy, ambiguous, human-centric space where data ends and judgment begin. If you are still leading from the predictable space, you are rapidly losing your strategic relevance.

To confront the truth of where your leadership is fragile requires vulnerability. AI holds up a mirror to your operating system and asks: *What is your unique, irreplaceable human value?* If your answer is "experience" or "process," your team will quickly seek leadership that is focused on vision, courage, and human connection—the qualities AI can only augment, never replicate. This is why *unlearning* must precede adoption. *When AI handles the transactional, what is left for you is the truly transformative.*

The Four Types of Leaders AI Will Expose

1. **The Controller:** (*Exposed by: Agentic Autonomy*) The leader whose value rests on their need to approve every decision. Agentic systems require trust and autonomy; the Controller will become a bottleneck that AI runs around, making the human irrelevant. Their need for involvement crushes speed.

2. **The Resister:** (*Exposed by: Exponential Speed*) The leader who delays adoption, prioritizes legacy systems, or fears the loss of old expertise. AI's speed will make their teams non-competitive almost overnight. The Resister's inaction will become competitive suicide.

3. **The Solver:** (*Exposed by: Analytical Power*) The leader who spends their time analyzing data and crafting solutions. AI is superior at this. The Solver needs to unlearn this habit and rewire to focus on *defining the right problems* and *cultivating human judgment.* Their value shifts from finding the answer to asking the right question.

4. **The Enabler:** (*The Rewired Leader*) The only type of leader who thrives. They unlearn the need for control and transactional oversight, focusing instead on mission clarity, coaching judgment, reinforcing culture, and ensuring the human-AI partnership drives ethical, high-speed outcomes.

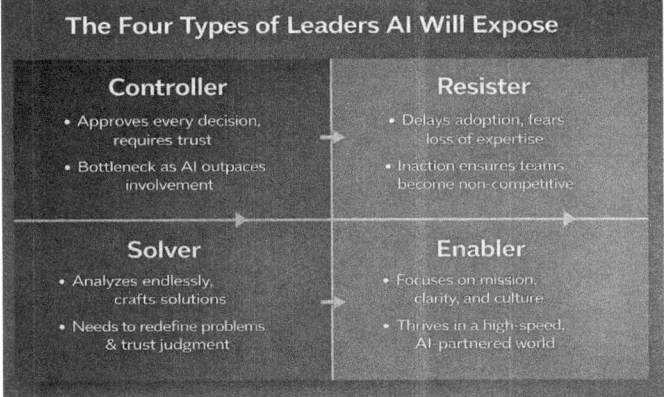

In a high-trust, *Rewired* environment, the leader trusts the team and the system to operate within clear guardrails. Their leadership bandwidth is freed up to focus on external market signals and ethical questions—the highest leverage activities.

THE AGENTIC REVOLUTION: REWIRING WORK, TEAMS, AND TRUST

If you think generative AI changed the way your teams search for information, you haven't seen anything yet. The truth is, that was the warm-up act. Your teams and your entire organization are about to confront the true reckoning: *agentic AI.* It is time to stop thinking about AI as a smarter intern and start seeing it as an autonomous team member.

The End of the Handoff Economy

As the CEO of an AI company, I have a distinct vantage point. I see the technical blueprints, but more importantly, I see the human friction those blueprints create inside the world's largest enterprises.

The shift is already happening in firms like Meta and Apple: they are moving from a *handoff economy* where work moves sequentially from one person or system to the next to an *agentic economy*. Agentic AI is designed not just to suggest an answer, but to *take action and achieve an outcome.* It doesn't ask for permission; it asks for a mission. This forces a complete architectural *rewire* of your organizational operating system.

The biggest casualty of agentic AI is the middle manager who only manages tasks. If your job is to coordinate handoffs, congratulations you are the last step before an autonomous system takes over. *Unlearn delegation by task and rewire for delegation by intent.*

The Failure of the Task Manager

Agentic systems expose the absurdity of traditional, linear task management. Why? Because the system works asynchronously and autonomously. It may run ten steps in parallel and then come back to you with a finalized proposal.

My observations from working with organizations like Intel show a clear pattern: when agentic systems are introduced, the most valuable employees are no longer the most organized executors, but the ones with the highest *adaptive intelligence*—the ability to deal with ambiguity and exercise high-stakes judgment.

The Ultimate Unlearning: Trust and Autonomy

This shift is profoundly human. When you delegate an outcome to an autonomous system, you are forced to confront the biggest leadership gap of our time: the gap between the *illusion of control* and the *mandate for trust.*

The *Rewired* leader understands that agentic AI is not a tool for surveillance or efficiency theater; it is a profound test of organizational culture. When trust is low, leaders instinctively over-engineer the agent's actions, adding layers of approval, excessive rules, and brittle controls that choke autonomy and drain value. When trust is high, leaders do something harder: they articulate intent, set clear missions and guardrails, and then step out of the way.

I saw this play out firsthand with a CEO who paused an agentic AI rollout days before launch. Not because the technology failed, but because she realized she was asking the agents to operate with more autonomy than she allowed her own leadership team. The question wasn't "Can we trust the agents?" It was "Have we created a culture where trust actually exists?" That moment reframed the entire initiative. The technology didn't change. The leadership posture did.

Rewiring a culture for agentic AI is ultimately about rewiring a leader's relationship with control, accountability, and risk. Agents don't just execute work; they reflect leadership behaviors already embedded in the system. They amplify clarity or confusion, confidence or fear. You don't scale intelligence by tightening your grip, you scale it by deciding what must be governed and what must be trusted. In that sense, agentic AI doesn't expose a technology gap; it exposes a leadership gap.

LEADERSHIP IS NO LONGER A ROLE—IT IS A SYSTEM

In modern organizations, leadership functions less like a personality and more like an *operating system.* An operating system determines how information flows, how decisions get made, what happens automatically, where humans intervene, and how exceptions are handled.

Leadership works the same way. Whether leaders intend it or not, they design the logic of the organization. They define what requires approval and what does not. They signal where judgment is expected and where compliance is rewarded. They create the guardrails within which work moves or stalls.

This is why changing leadership behavior without changing leadership design rarely works. You can coach better communication. You can train better managers. But if the underlying leadership system remains the same, the organization will revert under pressure.

Rewired Leadership™ begins when leaders recognize that their primary job is not to manage people, but to design how leadership works at scale.

WHY HUMAN SKILLS MATTER MORE THAN EVER

Over the past couple of years, I've spent time with senior leaders inside some of the most sophisticated organizations in the world. These are CEOs and executive teams with access to the best data, the best technology, and increasingly, powerful AI systems embedded into their operations.

And yet, the moments that slow them down are not technical. *They are human.*

I've watched an executive stare at a dashboard filled with real-time insights customer sentiment, operational signals, and predictive recommendations, and they hesitate. Not because the data wasn't clear, but because the decision carried ambiguity. Trade-offs. Consequences that couldn't be fully modeled.

In that moment, no system could decide for them.

What mattered was *judgment.* The ability to sit with uncertainty. The confidence to move without perfect information. The trust they had built with their team to act once the decision was made.

That's when it became obvious: as work becomes more automated, leadership becomes more human.

As AI accelerates coordination, analysis, and execution, the value of uniquely human capabilities increases. In a slower world, authority and experience were often enough. In today's environment, those signals no longer scale on their own.

What scales instead are human skills that technology cannot replace:

- Judgment
- Grit
- Curiosity
- Trust
- Resilience

These are not soft skills. *They are scaling skills.*

THE SHIFT THAT CHANGES EVERYTHING

The most important leadership shift in this era is subtle, but profound: Leadership is no longer about being the smartest person in the room. It is about designing the room so smart decisions happen everywhere.

That shift requires unlearning habits that once felt essential. It requires restraint. It requires trust. And it requires leaders to accept a difficult truth: What made you successful may no longer scale. That realization is uncomfortable. It is also the beginning of rewiring. The leadership rewire is not optional. It is the work of this era.

Chapter 2

The Leadership Gap No One Wants to Admit

MOST ORGANIZATIONS SENSE THAT something is off. They feel it within stalled initiatives. They see it in meeting overload. They experience it in frustrated teams and exhausted leaders. But very few are willing to name the real issue.

The problem is not talent. It is not effort. It is not technology.

The problem is a growing gap between how leaders were trained to lead and how work actually gets done today.

This gap doesn't announce itself. It doesn't show up as failure. It shows up as *friction*—small delays, repeated conversations, and decisions that take just a little longer than they should.

Over time, those delays compound.

HOW THE GAP FORMED

Most senior leaders came up in a different operating environment. Work was slower. Information was scarcer. Decisions were episodic. Authority flowed clearly up and down the organization.

Leadership behaviors evolved accordingly. Good leaders were expected to be deeply informed, review important decisions, ensure alignment before action, and manage risk through oversight. These behaviors were not wrong. They were contextually correct. But they were built for a world that no longer exists.

Today, work is continuous. Signals surface in real time. Teams operate across functions, geographies, and platforms. AI and automation compress cycles that once took weeks into hours or minutes.

Yet many leadership systems still assume decisions should be escalated, alignment should precede action, and leaders should be involved early and often.

That mismatch is the *leadership gap*.

WHAT THE GAP LOOKS LIKE IN PRACTICE

The leadership gap rarely shows up as incompetence. It shows up as *over-functioning*.

- Leaders attend too many meetings because they don't trust decisions will move without them.
- Teams hesitate because they are unclear where authority truly lives.
- Managers escalate decisions not because they need help, but because the system has trained them to.
- Everyone is working hard. Progress feels slow.

I've seen this play out repeatedly with executive teams who are genuinely committed to transformation. They invest in new platforms, new tools, and new operating models yet the experience on the ground barely changes.

Why? Because leadership behavior never rewired to match the new reality.

THE COST OF THE LEADERSHIP GAP

The cost of this gap is higher than most leaders realize.

First, it erodes momentum. Decisions get reviewed instead of resolved. Second, it drains leaders. Senior executives become the system's shock absorbers, absorbing complexity that should be distributed. Third, it disengages teams. High performers don't leave because of workload. They leave because of friction and lack of ownership. Most damaging of all, the leadership gap undermines the very transformations leaders are trying to drive. AI initiatives stall. Agile programs feel performative. Digital transformation delivers tools, not outcomes.

The technology is ready. The organization is capable. The leadership model is lagging.

THE SILENT SHIFT LEADERS MUST MAKE

Closing the leadership gap does not require leaders to care less. It requires them to lead differently.

The shift is subtle but profound:

- From solving problems → to designing systems that solve problems
- From making decisions → to designing decision rights
- From ensuring alignment → to creating clarity
- From managing execution → to enabling flow

This shift is uncomfortable because it challenges identity. Many leaders built their careers on being the person who steps in when things get hard.

Rewired Leadership asks a harder question: What if the organization didn't need you to step in at all?

Naming the Gap Is the First Step

This chapter is not an indictment of leaders. It is an acknowledgment of reality. Naming the gap is the first step toward closing it. The chapters ahead will explore how this gap plays out as work accelerates, how AI amplifies it, and how leaders can redesign their role to regain leverage. But first, leaders must be willing to admit the truth: The way leadership worked before will not carry us forward. And that realization, while uncomfortable, is also an opportunity.

Chapter 3

The Rewired CEO: Leading at the Intersection of AI, People, and Performance

THE ROLE OF THE CEO IS BEING STRUCTURALLY redesigned. It is no longer enough to be a great allocator of capital—you must be a great allocator of *attention* and *organizational energy.* Where previous CEOs focused on managing structure and resources, the *Rewired* CEO must manage the *speed of adaptation* and the *quality of human insight.*

The new reality is that the biggest drag on growth is no longer the market or the competition—it's *organizational friction.* Legacy leadership habits—slow decision loops, unnecessary layers of approval, and a culture of risk-aversion are the silent killers of enterprise value. The *Rewired* CEO recognizes that their primary job is to eliminate this friction and establish a high-performance operating system that is fundamentally human-centered, yet AI-enabled.

THE CEO'S DOUBLE BIND: STRATEGY VS. SYSTEM

The CEO faces a paradox that no other leader does: the crushing demand for quarterly results versus the existential imperative of long-term cultural transformation.

It is easy for a CEO to define a new strategy—a Power-Point presentation, a market announcement, an acquisition. But strategy is useless if the organization's operating system—its culture, its habits, and its leadership model—is built for a slower world.

The CEO's challenge is not *what* to change, but *how* to change the organizational system without sacrificing short-term performance. This means the CEO must become the "chief system architect" of the company's internal dynamics. They must be the one to identify and decommission the legacy habits—the unlearning debt—that threaten the new strategy.

If the CEO continues to lead by checking every decision, the organization will move at the speed of the CEO's inbox. This systemic reliance on one individual is the clearest sign that the leadership system is broken. The *Rewired* CEO must stop being the bottleneck and start being the relentless driver of *flow*.

REWIRED STRATEGY: THE ENTERPRISE VALUE OF ADAPTIVE INTELLIGENCE

For decades, the CEO's primary levers for value creation were financial: capital allocation, operational efficiency, and mergers and acquisitions (M&A). Today, the most valuable lever is *adaptive intelligence*—the organizational capacity to learn, unlearn, and respond to signals faster than the market.

Adaptive intelligence is not a soft skill; it is a measurable key performance indicator (KPI) directly linked to enterprise value.

- **Valuation Model Shift:** *Rewired* investors no longer reward size and stability alone; they reward speed and optionality. A culture burdened by friction is a liability in a world of exponential change. The CEO positions their commitment to unlearning and speed as a core competitive advantage.
- **Talent Flow:** The best talent—the people with the high-stakes judgment needed to partner with agentic AI—will only stay in environments that grant high autonomy and high clarity. The CEO must consciously design the culture to attract and retain these "rewired employees," viewing their retention not as an HR metric, but as the preservation of essential corporate intellectual property (IP).

The CEO must unlearn the notion that culture is a separate initiative run by HR. *Culture **is** the leadership operating system.* When that system lacks clarity and trust, it produces fear, which is the slowest and most expensive emotion in any business. The strategic goal of the *Rewired* CEO is to replace that fear with trust and clarity, transforming culture from a defensive mechanism into an accelerator of growth.

THE CEO'S PERSONAL UNLEARNING: THE HIGHEST-LEVERAGE HABIT

If the CEO is not visibly and relentlessly unlearning, no one else in the organization will take the risk. Transformation must be modeled at the top, or it remains merely an aspiration.

The first step in *Rewired Leadership*™ at the top is to unlearn the need for control. You must pivot from being the chief *problem-solver* to the chief *system architect*. Your job is to build the environment where the best ideas can surface, where talent is motivated by mission, and where the culture moves at the speed of the market. This requires a profound personal unlearning of the very habits that earned you the corner office.

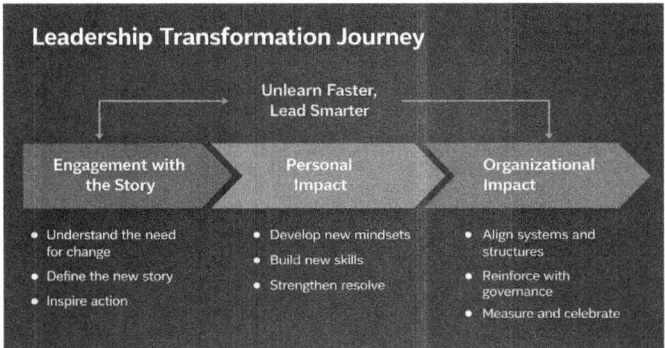

THE CEO AS CHIEF COMMUNICATOR AND COACH

The traditional communication style—the top-down directive, the fully scripted presentation, the demand for exhaustive detail—is a relic of the slow system. The *Rewired* CEO unlearns this habit and becomes the organization's "chief executive coach." Their primary communication leverage shifts from conveying *solutions* to reinforcing *intent* and *judgment*. This means communicating with extreme clarity on the *why* (the mission), defining the ethical guardrails, and then coaching managers to handle the *how*. By speaking less as the final authority and more as the chief facilitator of learning, the CEO effectively scales leadership development throughout the enterprise.

The most difficult habit for the successful CEO to unlearn is *certainty*. The CEO's office is often the loneliest because everyone expects the person in that chair to have the answer. The *Rewired* CEO must display the vulnerability to say: "I don't have the map, but I know the process, and I trust this team."

By modeling curiosity over confidence, and clarity over control, the CEO gives the entire organization permission to experiment, fail fast, and pivot rapidly. This intentional display of adaptive leadership is the single highest-leverage move a CEO can make to accelerate the organizational rewire.

Chapter 4

The Moment Every Leader Faces: When What Made You Successful Stops Working

THERE IS A MOMENT IN EVERY LEADER'S career that no one prepares you for. It doesn't arrive with drama. There's no announcement. No performance review tells you it's happening. It shows up quietly.

You're working harder than ever. Your calendar is full. You're in more meetings, closer to the details, and more involved in decisions than at any point in your career. And yet, the organization feels slower, not faster.

Decisions stall. Issues resurface. Teams hesitate.

And the most unsettling part is this: the instincts that made you successful for decades no longer seem to work the way they used to. This is the leadership moment few talk about and nearly every experienced leader eventually faces.

THE SUCCESS TRAP: WHEN ACHIEVEMENT BECOMES INERTIA

We call this phenomenon the "success trap." It is the perverse moment where your cumulative expertise and past victories create the cognitive inertia that prevents future adaptation. You are successful because you excelled in a certain environment, mastering its rules, processes, and pacing.

The world has changed those rules, but your leadership reflexes have not.

The leader in the success trap is battling an internal conflict: a profound sense of responsibility drives them to get closer to the work, while the reality of the faster system ensures that their involvement only creates drag. It's the ultimate cognitive dissonance: *My effort is high, but my impact is shrinking.*

WHEN STRENGTH BECOMES CONSTRAINT

For most of their careers, successful leaders are rewarded for stepping in. They unblock teams. They make the call. They bring clarity when others hesitate. Presence becomes power.

Over time, organizations adapt around this. People learn when to escalate. Meetings get scheduled "just in case." Decisions migrate upward because it feels safer.

What once felt like leadership gradually becomes *dependency.*

The leader becomes indispensable and unintentionally, the constraint.

This shift is subtle. It doesn't feel like failure. It feels like responsibility. Leaders step in because they care. Because they want to help. Because they believe involvement equals impact. But as work accelerates, that equation breaks down.

THE QUIET SIGNALS LEADERS MISS

Unlike past eras, leadership misalignment today rarely announces itself through crisis. Instead, it shows up quietly:

- Teams wait instead of deciding.
- Meetings multiply without resolution.
- Leaders feel exhausted but less effective.
- Momentum slows despite constant activity.

From the outside, the organization still looks functional. From the inside, everything feels heavier. This is not incompetence. It is misalignment. Leadership habits built for a slower system are now creating friction inside a faster one.

THE CASE STUDY: THE GLOBAL 100 WHO COULDN'T SCALE

Several years ago, I began working with a Global 100 technology firm, specifically with their CHRO, "Sarah." Sarah was, by every measure, a phenomenal executive: insightful, deeply experienced, and fiercely protective of her talent. Her mandate was to drive a critical, multi-year leadership transformation across 80,000 employees to prepare for their pivot to an agentic operating model.

The strategy was sound, the funding was there, and Sarah was working seventy-hour weeks. Yet, we hit a wall six months in. Key regional initiatives were stalled, not because of local resistance, but because the global executive committee (ExCom) was failing to *move out of the way*.

Sarah and I analyzed the data. The ExCom's average time for reviewing and approving regional transformation budgets—budgets pre-approved by their CFO—was forty-five days. The lag was attributed to "due diligence," but the real cause was deeply entrenched: every ExCom member, including the CEO, felt compelled to "add value" by suggesting minor modifications, inserting new metrics, or reviewing the process steps they already trusted their teams to handle.

Sarah eventually articulated the problem perfectly: "My leaders are drowning in the effort of being indispensable." Their need for personal involvement—the habit that got them promoted—was now the single biggest threat to the company's future speed. They were acting as expert reviewers, not system architects.

Our breakthrough came when Sarah challenged the CEO to publicly *unlearn* one high-friction habit. The CEO chose to stop reviewing *how* budgets were spent and focus solely on the *clarity of the intent* and the *ethical guardrails* of the investment. It was a small shift in behavior that immediately freed up over five hundred hours of executive time globally and signaled a profound change in leadership trust.

This proved the core thesis: transformation fails not from strategy, but from the inability of successful leaders to unlearn their role.

AI, DATA OVERLOAD, AND THE EROSION OF JUDGMENT

The arrival of agentic AI dramatically accelerates the leader's internal crisis. AI does not just provide information; it delivers the *certainty of the past*. It synthesizes millions of data points instantly, offering predictive probabilities and optimized recommendations.

The leader is presented with *perfect data at hyper-speed*. And yet, the decision pauses.

Why? Because the data often reveals three equally plausible, high-risk paths, or it flags an ethical ambiguity that the algorithm cannot compute. The moment requires *human judgment*—the ability to sit with uncertainty and weigh the trade-offs without perfect information.

This is where the old habit of "I must be deeply informed" fails. The leader, drowning in AI-generated data, reverts to the old playbook: calling more meetings, running more analysis, seeking more alignment. They are looking for the data to relieve them of the burden of judgment.

Ironically, AI's analytical superiority exposes the leader's *judgment deficit*. The leader's internal noise (their fear of ambiguity) clashes with the system's clarity, forcing the organization to wait.

THE COST TO THE ORGANIZATION: LOST LEVERAGE

The organizational cost of this erosion is significant. AI investments underperform. Automation accelerates tasks but not outcomes. High performers disengage silently. Decision cycles stretch.

Most damaging of all, *leverage is lost*.

In the old model, the leader's leverage was their knowledge and control. In the *Rewired* model, the leader's leverage is their *ability to design a system that amplifies the judgment of others*. When a leader steps in too often, they are stealing that opportunity for judgment from their team. The organization becomes dependent on leadership presence instead of leadership design. This is not sustainable.

THE CROSSROADS

The leadership moment is not a crisis. It is a crossroads.

One path leads to exhaustion, diminishing impact, and quiet irrelevance. The other leads to leverage, clarity, and resilience. The difference is not effort. It is design.

Leaders who recognize this moment early can rewire how leadership works before the cost of waiting becomes too high.

They redesign decision rights, create guardrails, and shift from managing execution to enabling flow. They move upstream.

The Real Work Begins Here: The Invitation to Unlearn

The painful realization that what made you successful may no longer scale is also the most liberating truth. It frees you from the burden of defending obsolete habits.

This chapter is an invitation to acknowledge that moment to stop blaming the technology, the teams, or the market, and to look inward at the system you lead. The hardest work in the *Rewire* framework is not learning new skills; it is *unlearning the habits of success.*

Leadership does not need to disappear. It needs to be rewired. And that realization is where the real work begins.

Chapter 5

Old Skills, New World

THE WORLD HAS CHANGED, BUT THE fundamental need for great leadership has not. What has changed is *where* leaders must apply their attention and *what* skills they must prioritize. The new world demands a leadership skill stack built on clarity, agility, and human connection.

THE AMPLIFICATION OF EMOTIONAL INTELLIGENCE (EQ)

As AI masters the domains of data, pattern recognition, and prediction (the domain of IQ), the unique human skills that drive organizational engagement, trust, and resilience become paramount. The value of emotional intelligence (EQ) is multiplied because it determines the quality of the human interactions left after the friction is dissolved.

The *Rewired* leader understands that their primary tool is no longer technical expertise, but *empathy and situational awareness.*

- **Self-Awareness (Unlearning the Ego):** The ability to recognize when their own habits (e.g., the need for control) are creating drag. This is the inner work of leadership rewiring.

- **Empathy and Social Awareness (Driving Trust):** The ability to read the unspoken fears of teams facing automation and to communicate with radical transparency. Low EQ creates fear, which kills speed. High EQ builds trust, which enables flow.

Leaders must *unlearn* the idea that success is built on technical genius alone. The most enduring leaders of the past—the Level 5 Leaders studied by Jim Collins in his book *Good to Great: Why Some Companies Make the Leap . . . And Others Don't*—were defined by a powerful mix of fierce resolve and profound personal humility. Their greatness was rooted in the ability to put the organizational mission above their own ego, a characteristic that is absolutely essential for leading in the age of autonomous systems.

THE REWIRED SKILL STACK: META-COGNITION IN LEADERSHIP

In the era of agentic AI, the most crucial leadership skill is not knowing the answer but knowing *how you know the answer*. This is *meta-cognition in leadership*: the ability to step back and analyze your own thinking and decision-making process.

AI gives you the result; the meta-cognitive leader questions the *assumptions* and the *system* that produced the result. This skill is the ultimate countermeasure to algorithmic bias and groupthink.

Skill 1: Clarity over Certainty (The Strategic Meta-Skill)

The *Rewired* leader unlearns the need to have all the answers. Instead, they become obsessed with *clarity of intent*. When agentic AI is making autonomous decisions, the mission and ethical boundaries must be crystal clear. Vague vision is no longer permissible.

- **The Unlearning:** The habit of waiting for 90 percent data certainty before making a decision. This comes from a fear of being wrong.
- **The Rewire: Intentional Ambiguity.** You explicitly define *what* is ambiguous and *why*, empowering the team to apply judgment within that zone while trusting the ultimate goal remains fixed.
- **Example:** Instead of mandating a specific marketing campaign channel (certainty), the *Rewired* leader defines the intent: "Increase lead conversion by 15 percent among the emerging small-to-medium business (SMB) segment while maintaining brand voice authenticity." This clarity allows the agentic system and the human team to iterate on the *how* at speed.

Skill 2: Coaching over Directing (The Relational Meta-Skill)

Rewired leaders unlearn the habit of giving prescriptive solutions. Instead, they focus on *coaching human judgment*. Your teams will be facing ambiguous problems AI can't solve; your job is to equip them to handle those problems with resilience and ethical weight.

- **The Unlearning:** The habit of "jumping in" to solve a team's problem immediately, thereby "stealing" the learning moment.
- **The Rewire: Scaling Judgment.** The leader's primary output is no longer a task list, but a higher-order question designed to force the team to confront ambiguity and weigh trade-offs.

- **The Test:** If you receive a decision proposal, do not edit the text or correct the analysis. Ask: *"What are the ethical trade-offs of option B?"* or *"What assumption in our model carries the highest risk if proven wrong?"* This trains the team to anticipate future consequences, the essence of high-value human work.

Skill 3: Speed over Perfection (The Execution Meta-Skill)

Rewired leaders unlearn the fear of failure and the pursuit of 100 percent certainty before launching. The market rewards speed and iteration. Speed is now a key performance indicator for culture. The faster the organization can pivot, the higher its competitive ceiling.

- **The Unlearning:** The habit of prioritizing polished, risk-mitigated final products over minimum viable products (MVPs) designed for learning.
- **The Rewire: Intentional Failure.** The leader creates a small, dedicated budget and cultural space for well-scoped experiments designed specifically to *fail fast.* The leader celebrates the insight gained from the failure, not the success of the outcome.
- **The Metric:** The organization measures *learning velocity* (how fast they move from insight to pivot), not just completion rates.

THE JOBS PARADOX: INTENSITY WITHOUT CONTROL

While figures like Steve Jobs were known for their uncompromising vision and intensity, their ultimate organizational success was less about their individual technical genius and more about their *EQ-driven ability to inspire radical loyalty and demand the absolute highest level of human judgment* from their specialized teams. Jobs was the ultimate "intent setter." He did not micromanage the code; he defined the experience and the uncompromising standard.

The modern leader must adopt Jobs's intensity for the *outcome* and the *customer experience*, while strictly *unlearning* the impulse to control the *process*—that is the work of the agentic system.

THE STRATEGIC IMPERATIVE: MANAGING HUMAN ENERGY

In the transactional economy, human energy was spent on execution and coordination. In the agentic economy, human energy must be conserved for *ambiguity, judgment, and connection.*

The *Rewired* leader recognizes that unnecessary complexity poorly defined processes, unclear reporting lines, and low-trust decision loops is the greatest drain on human energy. Every minute a high-value team member spends navigating internal friction is a minute they are not applying judgment to a market problem.

This demands a ruthless focus on *organizational simplification.* The leader must *unlearn* the tolerance for complexity, viewing it as a hidden tax on the profit and loss statement (P&L). By eliminating unnecessary steps and approvals, the leader strategically reallocates human energy from transactional tasks (which AI can handle) to transformative judgment (which only humans can provide). This is the highest form of leadership leverage in the AI era.

THE LEADER'S BEHAVIORAL REWIRE: A SUMMARY

The skills detailed above: clarity, coaching, and speed do not happen by accident. They require the conscious unlearning of deeply ingrained executive habits. The following table summarizes how the *Rewired* leader chooses to act and behave every day:

Leadership Challenge	The Old Behavior (To Unlearn)	The New Behavior (To Rewire)
Handling Mistakes	Punishes failure to prevent recurrence; seeks to identify blame.	Rewards *learning* from failure; seeks to identify *systemic assumptions* proven wrong.
The Role of Data	Demands 100% data certainty before making a decision.	Defines risk tolerance, uses AI for prediction, and applies *human judgment* to the ambiguity that remains.
Defining Work	Gives prescriptive tasks and detailed process instructions.	Defines clear, high-level *intent* and grants radical autonomy for the *how*.
Focus of Effort	Spends time on execution review, tracking, and process adherence.	Spends time on *coaching judgment*, designing guardrails, and enforcing ethical boundaries.
Organizational Signal	*Control* is the highest virtue; creates dependence.	*Trust* is the highest virtue; creates leverage and speed.

This behavioral summary serves as the foundation for the entire framework. It shows the leader that rewiring is not just a strategic choice—it is a moment-to-moment commitment to a new way of leading, thinking, and acting.

Chapter 6

Designing for Speed, Judgment, and Trust

SPEED HAS BECOME ONE OF THE MOST misunderstood leadership goals. Most leaders say they want faster decisions. What they often mean is faster execution after approval. That distinction matters.

In modern organizations, speed does not come from pushing people harder or compressing timelines. It comes from designing decision flow, so work does not have to wait.

Rewired leadership understands a simple truth:

- Speed without judgment creates chaos.
- Judgment without speed creates irrelevance.
- Leadership today must be designed for both.

WHY APPROVALS KILL SPEED

Approvals feel safe. They reduce personal risk. They create a paper trail. They signal responsibility. But approvals come at a cost. Every approval adds latency. Every review introduces hesitation. Over time, organizations trained on approval learn to wait instead of think.

The irony is that approvals often reduce decision quality. By the time a decision reaches leadership, context has faded and urgency has shifted. Leaders are forced to react to summaries instead of reality.

Rewired leaders replace approvals with clarity.

GUARDRAILS OVER PERMISSIONS

Guardrails are the foundation of speed with judgment.

Rather than asking teams to seek permission, leaders define the conditions under which teams are free to act. Guardrails clarify boundaries while preserving autonomy.

Effective guardrails answer questions like:

- What risks are acceptable without escalation?
- What decisions require consultation but not approval?
- What outcomes matter more than process?

When guardrails are explicit, teams move faster and make better decisions. Judgment improves because responsibility is clear. This is not a reduction in control. It is a redesign of it.

LEADERSHIP EXAMPLE: COMMANDER'S INTENT AND DISTRIBUTED CONTROL

The strategic rationale for guardrails over permissions is most clearly demonstrated in high-stakes, fast-moving environments. Consider the philosophy put forth by General Stanley McChrystal in his work on the military transformation captured in *Team of Teams: New Rules of Engagement for a Complex World.*

McChrystal realized that traditional, centralized command-and-control could not match the speed of a decentralized enemy. His solution was to *unlearn* the need for full situational awareness and control at the top. Instead, he championed "commander's intent." The leader communicates the *purpose* and the *desired end state* with absolute clarity (the intent and the guardrails) and then pushes the authority to make real-time decisions down to the individual operator closest to the action.

The goal was not to make perfect decisions—it was to make *fast, good-enough decisions* and trust the decentralized system to self-correct. For the *Rewired* leader, this means delegating 95 percent of the *how* to your agentic systems and human teams, allowing you to focus your scarce attention on the 5 percent of decisions that require pure, ethical judgment.

TRUST IS NOT A VALUE—IT IS A SYSTEM OUTPUT

Many leaders say they want trust. Few design for it.

Trust does not emerge from slogans or speeches. It emerges from systems that consistently reward good judgment and honest mistakes. When teams know the rules, trust grows. When leaders intervene unpredictably, trust erodes.

Rewired leaders understand that trust is built structurally. They:

- define authority clearly
- reinforce decision ownership publicly
- respond to mistakes with learning, not punishment

Over time, trust compounds. Speed follows.

JUDGMENT AS THE NEW LEADERSHIP CURRENCY

As AI and automation handle more routine decisions, human judgment becomes the scarce resource.

Rewired leaders focus their energy where judgment matters most:

- ambiguous trade-offs
- ethical decisions
- long-term consequences
- system design

They stop micromanaging execution and start coaching judgment. This is a profound shift. Leadership influence no longer comes from being involved everywhere. It comes from shaping how others think and decide.

WHAT SPEED REALLY LOOKS LIKE

In *Rewired* organizations:

- decisions happen closer to the work
- escalation is rare and intentional
- leaders intervene only when judgment truly matters
- teams move with confidence, not fear

Speed becomes sustainable because it is built into the system. This is what allows organizations to adapt continuously without burning out leaders or teams.

DESIGNING FOR THE FUTURE OF WORK

As work continues to accelerate, leadership design will matter more than leadership presence. Agentic systems will initiate tasks. Automation will handle coordination. AI will surface options instantly. Leadership that relies on approval, review, and constant involvement will collapse under this weight. Leadership designed for speed, judgment, and trust will scale.

THE LEADERSHIP CHOICE

Leaders have a choice. They can cling to control and become the bottleneck. Or they can design systems that allow others to move with clarity and confidence.

Rewired leadership chooses design over control, trust over permission, and judgment over oversight. That choice defines whether leadership becomes a constraint—or a multiplier—in the era ahead.

Chapter 7

Reset and Reframe: How Leaders Rewire the System Without Breaking It

EVERY LEADERSHIP TRANSFORMATION BEGINS with an uncomfortable realization. Not that something is broken, but that something no longer works the way it used to. This is the moment most leaders feel first, long before they can explain it. The organization is busy, but progress feels slower. Decisions are being made, but momentum is inconsistent. Meetings multiply, yet clarity feels elusive.

Leaders respond the only way they know how. By doing more. More involvement. More review. More availability. And that is exactly the problem. This habit of *over-involvement* is the primary driver of the Leadership Gap.

THE LEADERSHIP MOMENT INSIDE THE SYSTEM

There is a moment, often quiet and often private, when a leader realizes that their presence is no longer accelerating the organization. *It is slowing it down.*

This moment rarely arrives as failure. It arrives as *fatigue.*

You are working harder than ever, yet your leverage feels smaller. Teams wait for your input even when they do not need it. Decisions come to you not because they require your judgment, but because the system has trained people to escalate.

Nothing is technically wrong. And yet everything feels heavier.

This is the leadership moment where rewiring begins. Not because leadership has failed, but because leadership has *outgrown the system* it is operating in.

PHASE 1: RESET – SEEING THE SYSTEM CLEARLY

The "reset" phase is the most counterintuitive step in leadership transformation.

When pressure increases, leaders instinctively accelerate. Reset asks leaders to *pause.* Not to disengage, but to observe without intervening. Reset begins with a simple but difficult question: Where am I unintentionally becoming the bottleneck? This is not about blame. It is about visibility.

Rewired leaders take time to see how leadership actually works inside their organization, not how it is described in org charts or strategy decks. They look for:

- decisions that routinely escalate
- meetings that exist "just in case"
- approvals that feel mandatory but add little strategic value
- teams that hesitate even when capable

What emerges is rarely a capability problem. It is a *design problem*—a system built to rely on the leader's outdated habits.

The Trap of Over-Involvement

Most leaders believe involvement equals responsibility. In a slower world, that was often true. In a faster, AI-enabled world, over-involvement creates *dependency.* It teaches teams to wait. It discourages judgment. It shifts accountability upward instead of outward.

Reset requires leaders to stop doing three things immediately:

1. Stepping into decisions too early
2. Attending meetings where their presence adds little strategic value
3. Solving problems their teams are capable of solving

This restraint feels risky. It is also essential. Reset is about creating space, not for chaos, but for redesign.

Why Reset Alone Is Not Enough

Some leaders get stuck here. They diagnose endlessly. They map processes. They observe patterns. And nothing changes. Awareness without redesign creates frustration.

Reset is not the destination. It is the prerequisite. Once leaders can see the system clearly, the real work begins.

PHASE 2: REFRAME – REDESIGNING LEADERSHIP FOR FLOW

The "reframe" stage is where leadership actually changes. This is the shift from managing execution to *designing decision flow.* The core question of this stage is simple: What decisions should move without me, and under what conditions?

This is where most leaders hesitate. Because redesigning decision rights feels like giving up control. But in reality, it is how leaders regain *leverage*.

From Approvals to Guardrails

Rewired leaders replace approvals with guardrails. Guardrails are explicit conditions that allow teams to act with confidence. They define boundaries while preserving autonomy.

Effective guardrails clarify:

- Which decisions teams fully own
- Which decisions require consultation (but not approval)
- Which decisions require escalation (the 5 percent zone)
- What outcomes matter more than process

When guardrails are clear, decisions move faster and improve in quality. *Clarity replaces control.*

Redesigning Decision Rights

Reframing leadership requires leaders to move decision authority closer to the work. This does not mean abdication. It means *intentional distribution.* Leaders remain accountable for outcomes, but they are no longer the point of execution. This is where leadership scale is created.

When decision rights are clear:

- Teams act without waiting
- Leaders focus on judgment, not throughput
- The organization learns faster

Reframing leadership is not about stepping away. *It is about stepping upstream.*

HOW LEADERS REWIRE WITHOUT LOSING CONTROL

The fear most leaders share, often silently, is this: *If I step back, things will break. Rewired* leadership addresses this fear directly.

Control is not lost when leaders step back. It is redesigned. Accountability increases when ownership is explicit. Risk decreases when boundaries are clear. Trust grows when leaders respond consistently.

Rewired leaders:

- Intervene rarely, but decisively
- Coach judgment instead of correcting outcomes
- Reinforce autonomy publicly
- Treat mistakes as system feedback

This is not chaos. It is disciplined leadership design.

A REAL EXECUTIVE SHIFT

I have watched leaders make this shift in real organizations, often with surprising results. Within weeks of resetting and reframing, decision velocity increases. Leaders regain time. Teams show confidence. Meetings disappear without being cancelled. Not because people work harder. Because leadership stops being the place where work waits.

One executive said it best: "I did not realize how much of the system was built around me until I stepped out of it." That realization is the beginning of scale.

THE SHIFT THAT MAKES EVERYTHING ELSE WORK

Reset and Reframe together create the most important leadership shift of this era:

- From presence to *leverage*

- From control to *design*
- From heroics to *systems*

Leadership stops being reactive and becomes architectural. This is the moment leaders stop asking *how do I keep up* and start asking *how do I design this so I do not have to*.

WHY THIS IS THE CHAPTER THAT MATTERS MOST

Everything else in this book builds on this chapter. Without Reset, leaders cannot see the problem clearly. Without Reframe, leaders cannot fix it. Together, they form the heart of *Rewired Leadership.*

This is not a mindset exercise. It is not a cultural aspiration. It is a practical, repeatable way leaders redesign how leadership works without breaking trust, losing accountability, or slowing the organization down. *Rewired Leadership* does not happen by accident. It is designed. And this is where that design begins.

Chapter 8
Technology as a Leadership Multiplier

THE GREATEST TECHNOLOGICAL BENEFIT OF the AI era is not automation—it is *leverage*. For decades, leaders have been told they must work harder and get closer to the data. This model is collapsing under its own weight.

Your job is no longer to manage the system; it is to master the leverage provided by the technology. The *Rewired* leader views every AI investment not as a cost-saving measure, but as a direct injection of *leverage* into their own leadership capacity.

THE UNBEARABLE WEIGHT OF CONTROL

The un-rewired organization creates a vicious cycle for its leaders: complexity generates more data, more data demands more review, more review creates bottlenecks, and bottlenecks slow the entire system. You are working harder than ever, but your impact is diminishing because you are trapped in the transaction-based review cycle.

AI is the only lever powerful enough to break this cycle. It does not just automate tasks; it scales the impact of human judgment by handling the massive, hidden volume of work that previously consumed your high-value attention.

THE LEADERSHIP LEVERAGE EQUATION: TIME X JUDGMENT

To understand the shift, we must define the new metric of leadership success. The only thing AI cannot reproduce is the quality of human judgment applied to ambiguous, high-stakes decisions. Therefore, the *Rewired* leader's leverage is a function of the time AI frees up:

Leverage = [Time Freed by AI] x [Quality of Judgment Applied to Ambiguity]

If AI frees up 40 percent of your operational review time, but you simply use that time to attend more non-critical internal meetings (low quality of judgment), your leverage remains near zero. The *Rewired* leader uses that freed time to elevate their thinking to the 5 percent of decisions that require pure, ethical, strategic judgment.

FUNCTION 1: SCALING JUDGMENT, NOT TASKS

The first function of technology as a multiplier is to elevate the ceiling of human performance. AI must take over the transactional work to force the human leader to focus on the transformative work.

1. From Reviewer to Designer

The old leader's habit was to create a fifty-page report—reporting data in a clear, concise document for later analysis. The *Rewired* leader uses AI to generate that report instantly, reviews it for accuracy, and focuses the majority of their attention upstream on *designing the systems and criteria* that guide the AI's actions.

- **The Transactional Work:** Collecting and organizing data for analysis.

- **The Transformative Work:** Designing the ethical guardrails, defining the key strategic *assumptions*, and deciding which market variables are non-negotiable for the agentic system.

AI handles the transactional, freeing the leader to concentrate on due diligence and the ethical and strategic integrity of the *design*. The leader stops being the expert reviewer and becomes the "chief system designer."

Client Example: Scaling Learning Judgment in a Global Transformation

I recently worked with the chief learning officer (CLO) of a major services firm that was undergoing a massive leadership upskilling mandate. Their old system was collapsing under the weight of *manual correlation*—they had to manually link course completion data, performance review data, and business unit outcomes to justify a $50 million learning budget. The CLO and her team were trapped in what I call the "transactional 95 percent"—the operational drag that consumes leadership functions with administrative, reporting, and validation work long before strategy (the 5 percent) ever enters the room. In this case, approximately 80 percent of this CLO's time was spent gathering, cleaning, and reporting data. The exact percentage matters less than the consequence: the overwhelming majority of leadership energy was being spent on justification instead of judgment.

The Rewire with AI

We implemented an agentic system that autonomously performed this correlation. It constantly scanned learning consumption, aggregated performance improvement data, and flagged which learning interventions had the highest measurable *impact velocity* on organizational goals.

The Shift in Leverage

- **Before:** The CLO spent thirty hours per month reviewing reports (low-leverage transactional work).
- **After (Leverage Applied):** The CLO now spends three hours reviewing a single, high-leverage dashboard. This dashboard doesn't just show consumption; it flags *strategic anomalies* (e.g., "The top-performing region is consistently ignoring the mandatory sales training, indicating the training may be misaligned with their local success factors").
- **The 5 percent Judgment:** The CLO's newly freed time is spent on the *5 percent judgment*— not reporting consumption but strategically challenging the design of the learning curriculum based on real-time, AI-flagged insight. She stopped being the reporter and became the "chief learning strategy architect," multiplying her strategic impact exponentially.

2. The Principle of Augmented Insight

AI is not just good at finding answers; it is exceptional at finding *weak signals and exposing biases.* When used correctly, AI does not just confirm what you already know; it challenges what you *think* you know.

The *Rewired* leader uses AI to:

1. **Generate Alternatives:** Produce high-quality options (A, B, C) that a human team might miss.
2. **Highlight Assumptions:** Explicitly list the top five hidden assumptions driving each recommendation (e.g., "This option assumes the competitor will not respond for ninety days").

3. **Surface Weak Signals:** Identify fringe data points—market trends, cultural shifts, or internal sentiment—that challenge the dominant organizational narrative.

The *Rewired* leader's job is not to choose the safest option, but to apply judgment to the most challenging, high-leverage insights the AI provides.

FUNCTION 2: SCALING CLARITY, NOT COMPLEXITY

The second function of technology as a multiplier is to act as an organizational anti-friction agent. In a traditional organization, only the CEO has visibility into *all* the systemic bottlenecks. But the CEO is too busy dealing with the bottlenecks to fix the system.

The AI-Enforced System

AI tools can monitor the internal flow of work—the rate of approvals, the latency between handoffs, and the frequency of rework and flag the human friction created by leaders who are not rewired.

- **Technology as a Mirror:** AI dashboards expose the average time the executive committee takes to approve projects that already met all success criteria. This data creates undeniable proof of the "success trap" and forces the leader to confront their own habits.
- **Technology as an Enforcer:** An agentic system can enforce the "guardrails over permissions" model (Chapter 6). If a manager tries to insert an unnecessary review step outside the defined guardrails, the system can flag it as a violation

of the speed mandate, forcing accountability
for adherence to the new operating system.

Technology must enforce organizational simplicity and speed. It provides the objective data required to hold leaders accountable to the *system* rather than to personal loyalty or subjective effort.

THE TECHNOLOGY TRAP

The most common mistake leaders make is using AI to *scale control*. The leader still fears delegation, so they use AI to monitor their teams in granular detail. This scales the micromanagement habit and destroys the high-trust culture that true agentic AI requires.

The *Rewired* leader unlearns this impulse. They view AI as a tool to *eliminate the need for micromanagement*, not to facilitate it. Their focus shifts from checking their employees' status to checking the health of the organizational system itself.

Technology is neutral. It will multiply whatever leadership style you feed it. If you feed it control, you will multiply friction. If you feed it trust and intent, you will multiply leverage and speed.

Chapter 9

The 90-Day Leadership Rewire – a Playbook for Leaders Operating in an Agentic AI World

UNDERSTANDING THE NEED TO REWIRE leadership is no longer the hard part. *Execution is.*

Most leaders agree something must change. Few know where to start without destabilizing the organization or losing credibility. The result is delay. And in an environment shaped by agentic AI, delay is not neutral.

Agentic systems do not wait. They initiate work, surface decisions, escalate exceptions, and compress time. Leadership that is slow, approval-based, or overly centralized becomes friction almost immediately.

The 90-Day Leadership Rewire exists to solve that problem.

This is not a transformation program or a reorganization. It is a disciplined leadership reset designed for a world where humans and intelligent systems work together, decisions surface continuously, and leadership must operate at a higher altitude.

Ninety days is not arbitrary. It is long enough to change behavior and short enough to maintain urgency. More importantly, it is the window in which leadership credibility is either reinforced or lost.

This playbook is for CEOs, CHROs, and senior leaders who must adapt now, not later.

WHY AGENTIC AI CHANGES THE LEADERSHIP EQUATION

Most leaders still think about AI as a tool that supports work. Agentic AI changes that assumption.

Agentic systems do not simply analyze or recommend. They act. They coordinate workflows. They escalate exceptions. They learn from outcomes. In effect, they become *participants* in how work gets done. This fundamentally alters leadership dynamics.

Decisions surface faster than leaders can manually review them. Coordination happens automatically. Bottlenecks become visible in real time. Leadership presence is no longer required for execution, but *leadership design* is required for alignment.

In this environment, leadership that relies on escalation, review, and constant involvement collapses under its own weight.

The 90-Day Leadership Rewire is how leaders redesign their role so that human judgment and machine execution reinforce each other instead of competing.

THE PRINCIPLES OF THE 90-DAY LEADERSHIP REWIRE

Before the timeline begins, four principles must be clear.

1. **Subtraction Before Addition:** *Rewiring* leadership is about subtraction before

addition. Most organizations do not need more process. They need less friction.

2. **Model the Change:** Leaders must model the change before expecting it from others. Teams watch behavior, not announcements.

3. **Mistakes Are Data:** Mistakes are part of the process. In an agentic environment, learning speed matters more than initial precision.

4. **Clarity Beats Certainty:** Leaders must move even when answers are incomplete, because work will move regardless.

With these principles in place, the rewire can begin.

DAYS 1 – 30: RESET – CREATING VISIBILITY IN AN AGENTIC SYSTEM

The first thirty days are about seeing reality clearly.

In an agentic environment, Reset is especially important because AI exposes leadership bottlenecks immediately. Where decisions stall, where approvals delay action, and where humans hesitate, the system reveals it.

What Leaders Must Do

During days 1 – 30, leaders must observe without intervening. Specifically, leaders should:

- Identify where decisions are escalated even though AI has already surfaced clear options.
- Notice where agentic workflows pause awaiting human approval.
- Track where leadership presence is required for work to move.

- Listen for hesitation driven by unclear authority, not lack of insight.

Leaders should ask: Why did this decision need me? What signal did the system surface that we ignored? What guardrail was missing?

What Leaders Must Stop Doing

Reset requires leaders to immediately stop three behaviors:

1. Stop overriding decisions simply because they feel unfamiliar.
2. Stop inserting themselves into AI-enabled workflows too early.
3. Stop rescuing work that is uncomfortable but not truly at risk.

Agentic systems don't just reveal learning; they create it, thus compressing learning cycles dramatically in the process. Leadership determines whether that learning becomes leverage or liability, amplified through trust or suppressed through control.

What Success Looks Like After Thirty Days

By the end of day thirty:

- Leaders have visibility into where AI and leadership collide
- Decision bottlenecks are mapped clearly
- Teams begin trusting signals surfaced by systems
- Leaders feel discomfort but gain insight

That discomfort is data.

DAYS 31 – 60: REFRAME – DESIGNING GUARDRAILS FOR HUMANS AND MACHINES

Reframe is where leadership design changes.

In an agentic environment, leaders must be explicit about which decisions machines can initiate, which humans must decide, and where escalation is required.

What Leaders Must Do

During days 31 – 60, leaders must:

- Redesign decision rights for AI-initiated workflows
- Define guardrails that allow agentic systems to act without delay
- Clarify where human judgment overrides automation
- Communicate intent repeatedly and consistently

Guardrails should clarify acceptable risk thresholds, decisions AI can execute autonomously, decisions requiring human judgment, and non-negotiable outcomes.

The Leadership Shift Required

Leaders must shift from reviewing outcomes to reviewing *decision logic.* Instead of asking, "Was this the right result?" they ask, "Was the decision made within the right boundaries?"

This preserves accountability while allowing speed.

What Success Looks Like After Sixty Days

By the end of day sixty:

- Agentic workflows move without unnecessary human friction

- Leaders are pulled into fewer but more meaningful decisions
- Teams trust both the system and *Rewired Leadership*
- Decision velocity increases materially
- Leadership begins to scale.

DAYS 61 – 90: REINFORCE – HOLDING THE LINE WHEN AI SURFACES RISK

The final thirty days determine whether the rewire lasts.

As agentic systems surface more decisions faster, leaders will be tempted to re-centralize authority when risk appears. *Reinforce is about resisting that instinct.*

What Leaders Must Do

During days 61 – 90, leaders must:

- Reinforce decision ownership publicly
- Respond to AI-surfaced exceptions with judgment, not control
- Intervene decisively but rarely
- Treat mistakes as system feedback

Consistency matters more than intensity.

Managing the Accountability Gap: The Perception of Disengagement

The greatest threat to the *90-Day Leadership Rewire* is not failure of strategy, but failure of perception. When leaders transition from transactional involvement to strategic design, the immediate internal fear is the *accountability gap: If I'm not in the details, who gets the blame for the 5 percent of things that go wrong?*

The external fear is the *perception trap*: peers and the board, accustomed to seeing the leader as the hero of execution, may mistake restraint for disengagement. *Rewired Leadership* requires the leader to proactively manage this transition, defending their new role as system architect.

Actions to Mitigate Personal Risk

The leader must shift their communication from demonstrating *effort* to demonstrating *design*. This requires specific, high-leverage actions:

1. **Change Your Language:** Stop using passive language like "I'm stepping back." Replace it with active, powerful statements focused on design: "My highest-leverage work now is designing the non-negotiable guardrails for this system," or "My intervention is reserved solely for ethical judgment calls, as intended by our new operating model."

2. **Report the System, Not the Task:** When reporting to the board or executive peers, do not discuss the progress of individual projects. Instead, report on the *health of the system* using your new dashboard metrics: "Decision cycle time is down 25 percent because the guardrails held firm this quarter," or "Our escalation rate dropped, proving our investment in decentralized judgment is paying off." This reframes your job from *doing the work* to *designing a system that works*.

3. **Conduct Strategic Autopsy:** When a mistake occurs (and it will), do not investigate was responsible. Instead, immediately ask: *"Which guardrail failed, and how do we design a new one?"* This models the new culture, protects the team, and

redirects accountability toward the system design (the leader's new domain) rather than human error.

By making the accountability for *system design* explicit, the *Rewired* leader elevates their personal risk from "blame for execution" to "responsibility for architecture"—a far more defensible and higher-value role.

What Success Looks Like After Ninety Days

By the end of day ninety:

- Leadership involvement is intentional, not habitual
- Agentic workflows operate with trust
- Escalations are deliberate
- Leaders operate at a higher altitude
- Leadership leverage increases
  because the system works.

DESIRED OUTCOMES AND THE LEADERSHIP DASHBOARD

Rewired leadership must be visible, measurable, and defensible. The following outcomes and dashboard indicators allow leaders, boards, and executive teams to assess whether the rewire is working.

Desired Outcomes

- Faster decision velocity without increased risk
- Reduced leadership involvement in routine decisions
- Increased team confidence and ownership
- Effective human and AI collaboration
- Leadership time redirected to strategy and judgment

Leadership Rewire Dashboard

Leaders should track:

- **Decision Cycle Time:** Average time from signal to decision, pre- and post-rewire.
- **Escalation Rate:** Percentage of decisions escalated to leadership unnecessarily.
- **Leadership Time Allocation:** Percentage of time spent on judgment and system design versus execution.
- **Agentic Workflow Throughput:** Number of AI-initiated actions completed without human delay.
- **Exception Quality:** Quality and relevance of decisions escalated to leaders.
- **Team Confidence Signals:** Survey or qualitative indicators of decision confidence and clarity.

When these indicators move in the right direction, *Rewired Leadership* is working.

THE OUTCOME OF THE 90-DAY LEADERSHIP REWIRE

After ninety days, leaders experience a fundamental shift.

They are no longer the center of execution. They are the *designers of how work moves.*

In an agentic world, this is not optional. Leadership that does not rewire will become the bottleneck. Leadership that does will become the multiplier.

This chapter is not about preparing for the future. *It is about leading it.*

Chapter 10
Learning Fast – The Engine of Adaptive Intelligence

THE ULTIMATE COMPETITIVE EDGE IN THE agentic AI era is not speed of execution; it is *speed of adaptation*. The *Rewired* leader understands that the organization must be built to pivot faster than the external environment demands. This requires shifting from a culture focused on knowing to a culture obsessed with *learning velocity*.

Adaptive intelligence is the core intellectual survival skill. It is the ability to rapidly *unlearn* obsolete assumptions, acquire new skills, and pivot the organizational model before the market forces the change.

THE PROBLEM WITH SINGLE-LOOP LEARNING

Most organizations are trapped in *single-loop learning*. When something goes wrong, a project fails, a metric dips, or a prediction is missed—single-loop learning asks, "How do we fix the error?" It focuses on correcting the immediate deviation without questioning the underlying system.

A single-loop culture prioritizes *certainty*. When a project fails, leaders ask, "Who made the mistake?" and "How do we prevent it next time?" The focus is on procedural compliance, which is now the domain of AI.

This approach is fatal in an agentic environment because AI is already solving single-loop problems. AI optimizes execution within defined parameters. The *Rewired* leader's mandate is to push the organization into *double-loop learning*.

A double-loop culture prioritizes *diagnosis*. When a project fails, leaders ask, "Why did our process, our assumptions, or our guardrails allow that mistake to occur?" The focus is on questioning the governing rules themselves.

- **Single-Loop:** Fix the outcome.
- **Double-Loop:** Fix the assumptions
  that shaped the system.

This is where human judgment applied to ambiguity truly matters. The organization must be designed to treat every mistake as feedback on its core operating philosophy, not just a failure of execution.

This shift is existential. If your culture cannot support double-loop learning, every mistake will only lead to more bureaucratic complexity, slowing the entire organization.

THE UNLEARNING MANDATE: CLEARING THE CACHE

Every organization carries obsolete mental models that slow it down. The hardest concepts to unlearn are the ones that led to past success—the "success traps" discussed in Chapter 4. These obsolete habits act as drag on the learning system. For the leader, unlearning means confronting the three major cognitive obstacles:

1. **The Ego of Expertise:** The belief that past mastery
   guarantees future relevance. The *Rewired* leader
   must model intellectual humility by explicitly
   stating what they need to unlearn this week.

2. **The Fear of Opportunity Cost:** The paralysis that prevents leaders from shutting down successful, but stagnant, initiatives. Unlearning requires the courageous subtraction of organizational effort.

3. **The Comfort of Certainty:** The cultural aversion to intentional ambiguity. Adaptive intelligence demands the capacity to operate effectively without a complete map, treating uncertainty as a constant, not an exception.

THE SHIFT: FROM KNOWLEDGE AUTHORITY TO CHIEF QUESTION OFFICER

In the age of generative AI, the leader is no longer the "chief knowledge officer." AI can synthesize information and provide answers with greater speed and breadth than any individual.

The leader's new role is to become the "Chief Question Officer."

The most powerful questions in a *Rewired* organization are those that challenge the system and force double-loop learning:

- "What data are we currently *ignoring* that, if proven true, would invalidate our core strategy?"
- "What process are we clinging to that exists only to manage a *risk that no longer exists*?"
- "Are we optimizing for efficiency (low cost) or for *learning velocity* (speed of pivoting)?"

By modeling radical curiosity and asking questions that demand systemic rethinking, the leader creates the space for teams to engage in high-leverage judgment rather than low-leverage execution.

THE THREE PILLARS OF LEARNING VELOCITY

Learning velocity is the metric that truly matters. It is defined as the time it takes for an organization to move from *recognizing the need for a change to implementing a refined model based on new insight.*

Rewired leaders manage learning velocity through three systemic pillars:

Pillar 1: Psychological Safety as a Pre-Requisite

Fast learning is predicated on high trust. If an employee believes surfacing a failure will result in punishment, the organization slows to the speed of the slowest cover-up. The leader must treat mistakes as data points for learning transformation, not endpoints for personal accountability. This requires modeling the three behaviors:

- **Own the System Failures:** When a decentralized decision goes wrong, the leader must take responsibility for the failed *guardrail* (Chapter 6), not the individual's *judgment.*
- **Decouple Error from Identity:** Ensure that discussing errors is viewed as a functional requirement for organizational health, not a flaw in character.
- **Incentivize Challenge:** Reward team members who surface data that contradicts the dominant leadership narrative.

Pillar 2: Intentional Exposure and Experimentation

Learning velocity accelerates when the organization is intentionally exposed to low-risk, high-feedback experiments.

The leader must *unlearn* the habit of launching only polished, fully vetted projects.

Instead, the organization should be running a continuous stream of *minimum viable experiences (MVEs).* These are small, controlled, time-bound efforts designed specifically to challenge a core assumption.

- **The Rewire:** Allocate 5 percent of the budget specifically for minimum viable experiences (MVEs) designed to fail within sixty days.
- **The Metric:** Measure the number of strategic assumptions validated or invalidated per quarter, not just project completion rates.

Pillar 3: Embedded Feedback Loops

Learning must be built into the workflow, not bolted on as a quarterly review. Technology must enable immediate feedback.

- **Agentic Feedback:** Utilize agentic AI to monitor decentralized decisions and immediately surface performance data back to the team (within hours, not weeks). This compresses the learning loop dramatically.
- **After Action Reviews (AARs):** Adopt the military practice of AARs—short, candid debriefs immediately following any significant action. The structure is simple: *What was supposed to happen? What happened? Why was there a difference? What will we do differently next time?* This institutionalizes double-loop learning.

LEADERSHIP EXAMPLE: SCALING LEARNING AT NETFLIX

No company exemplifies high-velocity learning better than Netflix. Their success was not built on having a static, brilliant strategy, but on designing a culture that could *unlearn* faster than its rivals.

Reed Hastings and his team famously championed "context, not control," a concept that directly aligns with the "guardrails over permissions" model (Chapter 6). This cultural context provided the bedrock for learning velocity:

- **Unlearning the Process:** They discarded overly prescriptive rules, instead giving massive responsibility to smart, high-performing individuals (trusting decentralized judgment).
- **Institutionalizing Candor:** Their culture of extreme honesty, including "keeper tests" (asking if a manager would fight to keep an employee), forced rapid, difficult learning about personnel and performance, accelerating necessary pivots.
- **Tolerating Product Failure:** They have publicly embraced massive content failures (e.g., specific series that didn't land) as the necessary cost of scaling their success rate. This deliberate tolerance for failure is the financial manifestation of high learning velocity.

The *Rewired* leader must design their organization not to resemble a perfect machine, but a highly resilient organism capable of continuous, rapid evolutionary change. This reliance on high-speed learning is the ultimate defense against the accelerating complexity introduced by agentic AI.

Chapter 11

The Rewire Plan – Making Rewired Leadership a Continuous Discipline

THE GREATEST RISK AFTER A SUCCESSFUL leadership rewire is believing the work is done. It isn't. *The 90-Day Leadership Rewire* (Chapter 9) creates momentum. The *Rewire* plan ensures that momentum compounds instead of fading. In a world shaped by continuous change, agentic AI, and accelerating decision cycles, leadership cannot be redesigned once and left alone. *Leadership must be maintained.*

The 90-Day Leadership Rewire is how leaders turn *Rewired* leadership from a moment into a *continuous discipline*.

THE FIFTH INDUSTRIAL REVOLUTION: WHY MAINTENANCE IS MANDATORY

We are not merely experiencing a cycle of technological innovation; we are navigating the early stages of the Fifth Industrial Revolution (Industry 5.0). While previous industrial revolutions focused on automating physical labor, this era centers on *intelligent automation and co-creation*—the seamless, dynamic partnership between human judgment and machine action.

Every few decades, a technological shift fundamentally restructures the global economy, rendering previous competitive advantages obsolete:

- **The First Shift (Personal Computer):** Decentralized *information*. Knowledge workers gained individual processing power, but central command structures still dictated how that power was used.
- **The Second Shift (The iPhone/ Mobile):** Decentralized *access*. Knowledge and communication became instantly mobile and ubiquitous.
- **The Third Shift (Agentic AI):** Decentralized *action*. Agentic systems don't just process or provide access; they initiate complex, multi-step actions autonomously. This shift decentralizes the point of execution itself.

This third shift, which powers Industry 5.0, means that the organization's speed limit is no longer the speed of its network or its centralized decision-makers; it is the speed of its *leadership design*. If the leadership system resists the autonomous speed of the agent, the entire organization becomes friction.

Without a discipline to revisit leadership design, organizations slowly drift back to old patterns. Escalations increase. Leaders reinsert themselves. Decision velocity slows. *The 90-Day Leadership Rewire* exists to prevent this regression.

THE DANGER OF NORMALIZATION OF DEVIANCE

The reason organizations drift is rooted in culture, specifically the concept of "normalization of deviance." This is the subtle, slow process by which previously unacceptable standards or risky habits become normalized and accepted as the new base-line for operation.

For example, a leader begins inserting themselves into 15 percent of routine decisions to "help." Because nothing immediately breaks, this 15 percent involvement becomes the new, acceptable norm. The system has drifted, and the leader has subconsciously reinserted a bottleneck, eroding the trust and judgment they worked ninety days to establish.

The 90-Day Leadership Rewire is the formalized counter-measure to this invisible drift.

CASE STUDY: THE COST OF COMPETITIVE DRIFT (THE KODAK PARADOX)

To understand the necessity of continuous self-correction, consider the fate of Kodak. Kodak was the inventor of digital photography. Yet their failure was not a technological one; it was a leadership failure.

The failure was rooted in a profound normalization of deviance around their business model. Their highly successful core business in film and chemicals became the unexamined guardrail. They could not accept the data signals suggesting the future was digital because their entire system was designed to optimize the *past*.

The internal organizational system repeatedly chose *preservation over adaptation*. Every signal that challenged the profitability of film was dismissed, normalized, or minimized. The leadership failure was the lack of a structured, disciplined review cycle of their own core *assumptions* (the system's rules). This lack of continuous self-correction led not to an accident, but to *competitive obsolescence*—the silent death of market relevance.

A PERSONAL LEADERSHIP EXAMPLE: THE THIRTY-FIVE-YEAR PATTERN

This pattern of internal self-destruction—the inability to unlearn and self-correct is the single most consistent failure point I have observed in my thirty-five years working with executive teams.

In the mid-2000s, I consulted with a major financial institution that had successfully delegated pricing decisions down to their regional branch managers (a massive move at the time, akin to today's agentic delegation). The system worked well, increasing local market speed. However, one regional CEO, terrified of the risk, never stopped reading every single pricing report, even after delegation.

He never issued a veto or a correction, but his regional managers *knew* he was watching. Within six months, the managers stopped taking risks that required judgment, instead making safe, committee-approved pricing recommendations—exactly what they thought the CEO wanted. The *systemic drift* was invisible: decision time slowed by 30 percent, not because the policy was wrong, but because the CEO's *behavior* (his failure to fully *unlearn* the need for control) reinserted the bottleneck.

The 90-Day Leadership Rewire is the antidote to this ubiquitous human habit. It forces leaders to audit their own behavior and the true, lived rules of the system, not just the official handbook.

THE QUARTERLY LEADERSHIP REWIRE CYCLE: FOUR DIAGNOSTIC QUESTIONS

At the core of *the 90-Day Leadership Rewire* is a simple, repeatable rhythm. Every ninety days, leaders step back and ask four questions. These questions are not theoretical. They are diagnostic and designed to challenge the new status quo.

1. Where Has Work Slowed? (The Friction Check)

The Stake: This question determines if the organization is prepared for the speed of the Industry 5.0. Friction in the system guarantees competitive failure.

Actions and Audit:

- **Audit Cycle Times:** Examine the dashboard data (Chapter 9) for decisions that exceeded the target cycle time by 20 percent or more. Look beyond the average; identify the *worst-case* latency decisions.
- **Investigate Escalation:** For every escalated decision, audit the underlying reason. If the reason is "unclear guardrails," the *system* failed. If the reason is "fear of judgment," the *culture* failed.
- **Leader's Self-Correction:** The leader must commit to immediately deleting one unnecessary approval step or one unnecessary recurring meeting that emerged during the quarter. This must be a visible, public act of subtraction.

Slowness is a signal. It often indicates unclear authority, outdated guardrails, or, most critically, *leadership involvement that has unintentionally crept back in.*

2. Where Have Decisions Drifted Upward? (The Control Check)

The Stake: This audit determines whether the leader has maintained the integrity of the guardrails and protected decentralized judgment. Upward drift is a silent trust killer.

Actions and Audit:

- **Review Communication Logs:** Use agentic tools to audit executive communication logs for informal control vectors—keywords like "Can you just run this past me?" or "I need to review this one exception."

- **Peer Accountability:** Executive team members must mutually agree to gently call out a colleague who exerts an informal veto or asks for unnecessary involvement. This enforces the executive team's shared accountability for system health.

- **Redefine the 5 Percent:** Conduct a session where the executive team jointly reviews the last five decisions escalated to them. If three of those decisions *could have been solved* by the team below, the 5 percent rule is leaking, and the guardrails must be tightened or the coaching improved. This is the continuous investment in team judgment.

Upward drift is natural. It is not a moral failure, but it must be corrected intentionally.

3. Where Is Automation Creating Friction? (The Agent Check)

The Stake: This audit ensures the co-creation partnership is effective. If the human-machine interaction is inefficient, the promise of Industry 5.0 is broken.

Actions and Audit:

- **Test the Guardrails:** Intentionally run a simulation where the agentic system operates near the boundary of a critical guardrail. Does the agent handle the complexity correctly? Does it escalate appropriately? The leader must proactively break the system in a controlled environment to stress test the design.

- **Audit Exception Quality:** Track the percentage of exceptions surfaced by the AI that were deemed "low value" by the executive. If the AI is sending low-value noise, the leader's *intent* for the AI is unclear or the AI's learning parameters are misaligned. This check is crucial for preserving the leader's time for high-value judgment.

- **Leader's Self-Correction:** Refine one specific AI output or data request to ensure it aligns perfectly with the current strategic intent, maximizing the leverage provided by the technology. The focus must be on improving the *quality* of the AI's collaboration.

The goal is not to maximize automation. It is to *align automation with leadership design.*

4. Where Are Leaders Over-Involved Again? (The Ego Check)

The Stake: This is the audit of the leader's personal *unlearning.* Failure here renders all other efforts meaningless.

Actions and Audit:

- **Measure Intervention Rate:** The leader must track their own intervention rate on delegated decisions. A high rate suggests the leader has not fully unlearned the habit of being the hero.
- **The Systemic Autopsy:** When a mistake occurs, the leader must publicly conduct a *systemic autopsy* (not a personnel review). This asks: "Which guardrail failed, and how do we design a new one?" This models the required behavior and protects the culture of judgment.
- **Commit to Subtraction:** The leader must publicly commit to the subtraction of one daily or weekly task they previously owned that can now be delegated to the system or a team member. This demonstrates that their true value lies in architecture, not throughput.

This is the hardest question. It is also the most important, as the leader's behavior is the ultimate systemic input.

THE DISCIPLINE THAT SEPARATES LEADERS

Many leaders can lead change once. Few can sustain it.

The leaders who thrive in this era treat leadership design the way elite organizations treat strategy. They revisit it. They refine it. They invest in it continuously.

The 90-Day Leadership Rewire is how *Rewired Leadership* becomes permanent. Not as a framework on paper. But as a discipline in practice.

Chapter 12

Culture as an Operating System

FOLLOWING *THE 90-DAY LEADERSHIP REWIRE,* leaders often pivot to focusing on technology or talent. But the hardest, most necessary work is maintaining the cultural infrastructure. Culture is not an aspiration; it is the *predictive result* of what your organization does when the leader is not looking. It is the invisible operating system that either amplifies the speed of agentic AI or neutralizes it. If the culture rewards control, the *90-Day Leadership Rewire* will fail. If the culture rewards centralized decision-making, the entire system will seize up.

The *Rewired* leader views culture not as soft HR policy, but as the hardest form of organizational engineering.

THE CULTURE-TECHNOLOGY PARADOX

In Industry 5.0, technology decentralizes *action*, but culture determines the safety and speed of that action.

- If the system gives a team autonomy, but the culture punishes failure, the team will refuse to use its autonomy.

- If agentic AI surfaces uncomfortable data, but the culture suppresses dissent, the data will be ignored.

Culture must be designed to maximize *adaptive intelligence*—the capacity to rapidly unlearn, learn, and pivot. Without this cultural engine, the continuous self-correction demanded by *the 90-Day Leadership Rewire* is impossible.

THREE CULTURAL GUARDRAILS FOR THE REWIRED ORGANIZATION

Rewired leaders install three explicit cultural guardrails to transform their culture into an operating system built for speed and adaptation.

1. The Guardrail of Candor: Truth over Harmony

The speed of organizational learning is limited by the willingness of people to speak uncomfortable truths. In most organizations, social harmony is prioritized over candor, especially when challenging a senior leader's decision.

- **The Rewire:** Institutionalize mechanisms that force candor. This means establishing systems like anonymous pre-mortems, red-teaming sessions, or mandatory devil's advocacy in decision meetings where dissenting views are not but for a decision to move forward.
- **The Metric:** The most powerful cultural metric is the : How often is a high-stakes decision challenged by a non-senior executive before approval? A low ratio is a red flag that harmony is overriding truth.

2. The Guardrail of Systemic Accountability: Process Over Person

A fear-based culture blames people. An adaptive culture blames the process. The failure to distinguish between these is the primary driver of low psychological safety.

- **The Rewire:** When an error occurs, the leader's first action must be to shield the individual and immediately initiate a *systemic autopsy*. The focus is: *Which guardrail failed?* not *Who made the error?* This reinforces that the leader is accountable for the system, and the team is accountable for operating within the system.
- **The Metric:** Track the *systemic autopsy rate (SAR)*: The percentage of significant errors that result in a documented change to a process or guardrail, versus those that result in a personnel action. A high SAR signals a healthy, learning culture.

3. The Guardrail of Intentional Ambiguity: The Quest for the Best Question

The greatest source of friction is the cultural obsession with having the *right answer*. In a fast-moving, agentic environment, the pursuit of the "final answer" is a time-wasting loop.

- **The Rewire:** Shift the cultural value from expertise to *curiosity*. Leaders must reward the individual who asks the *best question*—the one that challenges a core assumption over the individual who provides the fastest answer. This cultivates the role of the "chief question officer" (as previously discussed).
- **The Metric – The Assumption Challenge Rate (ACR):** The number of core strategic assumptions explicitly challenged and

documented in high-stakes meetings per quarter. High ACR means high adaptive capacity.

EXECUTIVE COACHING MOMENT: THE CULTURAL INTERVENTION

The true test of *the 90-Day Leadership Rewire* success is not found in a metric, but in a crisis of faith the moment when a manager, operating under stress, violates one of the new cultural guardrails.

I have found that these cultural violations happen constantly, requiring the leader to be "on" all the time, not as a reviewer, but as a *cultural intervenor*.

I was working with the CEO of a major logistics firm who had successfully implemented the systemic accountability guardrail. Six weeks later, a key shipment was mishandled by a junior team, costing the company a significant amount. The senior VP of operations immediately violated the new system by scheduling an all-hands meeting to "find out who dropped the ball."

The CEO's intervention was simple, immediate, and public. This was a *coaching moment:*

"I called the VP and said: 'I see what you're doing. You're trying to fix the problem by looking for a person to blame. You are violating the systemic accountability rule we just installed. You are telling your entire organization that the rule doesn't apply when the stakes are high. *You have one hour to cancel that meeting and replace it with a systemic autopsy session.* You need to publicly state that this failure is a design flaw, not a personnel flaw, and you will be leading the redesign. Do not speak to the team until you have changed the question from *Who?* to *Why was our guardrail too wide?*"

This kind of cultural intervention—immediate, zero-tolerance for regression, and focused entirely on the *system*—is what cements the new operating system. It proves that the culture is the ultimate guardrail. The leader must be ready to intervene culturally *all the time*, because the old system is always fighting to return.

CULTURE AS AN ANTI-FRICTION ENGINE

In the agentic AI era, cultural friction is a direct competitive liability.

The cultural obsession with formal approval, the fear of dissenting, and the pressure to deliver certainty are all anti-friction agents that slow work and kill adaptive intelligence.

The *Rewired* leader designs their culture for *flow*:

- **Trust replaces formality:** The expectation of decentralized judgment eliminates the need for endless sign-off layers.
- **Action replaces analysis:** The clarity provided by the guardrails makes it safe for teams to act with confidence.
- **Learning replaces blame:** The systemic autopsy ensures that errors become productive system upgrades rather than personal liabilities.

Ultimately, culture is the infrastructure that allows the organization to achieve the ultimate goal: *scale*. You cannot scale without trust, and trust is the highest function of a well-designed culture.

THE TRUE COST OF A STATIC CULTURE

The leaders who fail to rewire their culture will find that their multi-million-dollar investments in agentic AI yield minimal return. The technology will deliver speed, but the culture will reject it. The data will deliver truth, but the culture will suppress it.

A static culture in an era of exponential change is a death sentence by a thousand small decisions. It is the failure to make the organization intellectually safe enough to confront the truth of its own obsolescence.

The *Rewired* leader knows that installing a high-velocity culture is the only way to future-proof their organization and ensure the continuous success of the *90-Day Leadership Rewire.*

DESIRED OUTCOMES: THE RETURN ON CULTURAL INVESTMENT

The *Rewired* leader recognizes that investing in a high-velocity culture is not a soft cost—it is the highest form of risk mitigation and the greatest driver of organizational leverage. When culture functions as a powerful, adaptive operating system, the following outcomes are the predictable result:

- **Sustained Decision Velocity:** The organization moves and pivots at the speed of the market, not the speed of its internal bureaucracy. The average time from identifying an opportunity to action drops significantly.
- **Reduced Friction Cost:** Time spent on unnecessary approval steps, formal reviews, and interpersonal conflict is dramatically reduced. This frees up high-value leader time (Chapter 8: the leadership leverage equation).
- **Decentralized Resilience:** Teams proactively challenge and refine guardrails without waiting for

executive intervention, preventing systemic drift and mitigating the risk of competitive obsolescence.

- **Accelerated Adaptive Intelligence:** Errors immediately translate into system upgrades, not fear. The organization's capacity for *double-loop learning* ensures that every mistake makes the organization smarter, faster, better.
- **High Talent Retention and Attraction:** Top talent—especially the emerging workforce—gravitate toward organizations where judgment is trusted, and the system is designed for flow, not friction.

By treating culture as the ultimate operating system, the *Rewired* leader ensures that their most sophisticated techno-logical investments and their most talented people can operate at their full potential, maintaining the continuous discipline demanded by the *90-Day Leadership Rewire.*

Chapter 13

The CHRO Playbook: Building the AI-Ready Organization

IN INDUSTRY 5.0 THE CHIEF HUMAN RESOURCES officer (CHRO) is no longer a strategic partner; they are the "chief transformation agent."

While the CEO champions the vision and the CTO manages the technology, the CHRO is the executive owner of the organization's *adaptive capacity*. It is the CHRO who must redesign the people systems the organizational structure, the talent pipeline, the metrics, and the incentives to ensure that agentic AI is implemented and utilized in the most effective manner. The CHRO must not only manage the transition but *lead the reinvention.*

I have spent the last decade, and over thirty-five years advising executive teams, working with *dozens of CHROs and their leadership teams* on how to best transform their organizations when confronting shifts like this. The consistent lesson is that every technological investment ultimately fails or succeeds based on the architecture of the people system.

THE NEW MANDATE: FROM COMPLIANCE TO CAPACITY

The traditional CHRO focuses on administration, risk mitigation, and talent acquisition. The *Rewired* CHRO must pivot to three core mandates:

1. **Validate Judgment over Activity:** Shift the entire performance system to measuring the quality of human judgment, not the volume of human activity.
2. **Architect Fluidity over Rigidity:** Design organizational structures that move at the speed of the agent, eliminating rigid job titles and silos.
3. **Incentivize Unlearning over Retention:** Use compensation and reward systems to encourage the difficult work of unlearning old skills and embracing systemic change.

This new mandate is the CHRO playbook for building the AI-ready organization.

PILLAR I: REWIRING TALENT MANAGEMENT – SKILLS AND JUDGMENT

In an agentic world, technical skills rapidly depreciate, but core human judgment becomes exponentially more valuable. The CHRO must lead the effort to identify, train, and measure these high-value human skills.

1. The Judgment Audit

The first step is a system-wide audit that maps human work to agentic potential. The goal is to isolate the *critical judgment moments* that cannot be automated.

- **Audit:** Map every core function's output to three categories: Execute *(Automate)*, Synthesize *(Augment)*, and Judge *(Isolate/Elevate)*.
- **Focus:** Training budgets must be aggressively shifted away from technical execution and toward *meta-cognition*—the ability to assess one's own decision process, manage uncertainty, and apply ethical guardrails. The CHRO owns making these previously "soft" skills the hardest, most measurable competencies in the organization.

2. The Unlearning Budget

The CHRO must institutionalize the concept of *unlearning*:

- **The Rewire:** Create an explicit *unlearning budget* and mandate its use. This budget funds time for high-value employees to deliberately *stop* performing obsolete tasks and focus on building new, high-judgment skills. This sends a powerful signal: the organization values future capacity more than current output.
- **The Talent Metric:** Measure the time to unlearn— the speed at which a high-value skill is replaced by an agent and the employee is successfully deployed into a new, higher-judgment role.

PILLAR II: REWIRING ORGANIZATIONAL STRUCTURE – FLUIDITY OVER RIGIDITY

Agentic AI systems disregard organizational charts; they create dynamic, cross-functional workflows. The organizational structure must reflect this reality, or it will become the single largest bottleneck.

1. Deconstructing the Job Title

Traditional job titles are administrative guardrails that restrict the movement of talent. The CHRO must move the organization away from static titles and toward *dynamic skill clusters or capabilities.*

- **The Rewire:** Define jobs based on *capabilities* (e.g., "critical risk assessor," "complex system integrator") rather than functional titles ("senior analyst"). This allows talent to be deployed fluidly across different agentic workflows as needs evolve.
- **The Structural Metric:** Track the talent mobility rate (TMR)—the percentage of employees who transition between significant capability clusters within eighteen months. A high TMR is a sign of structural health and resilience.

2. The Adaptive Organizational Design

The rigid, hierarchical org chart (designed for efficiency in the twentieth century) is incompatible with the speed of agentic execution.

The Rewire: The CHRO must champion the shift to *federated or modular organizational designs.* These structures distribute accountability and decision rights based on the guardrails, enabling self-correcting teams. This is how the CHRO embeds the *Reset and Reframe* concepts (Chapter 7) into the company's DNA. This means the CHRO often becomes the architect of a flatter, faster organization.

PILLAR III: REWIRING COMPENSATION AND INCENTIVES

Nothing reinforces old behavior faster than an outdated compensation system. The CHRO must align rewards directly with the behaviors required by *Rewired* leadership.

1. Rewarding System Health, Not Individual Output

In the agentic era, individual output is heavily augmented by the machine. Rewarding volume incentivizes teams to override the agent.

- **The Rewire:** Compensation models must shift from rewarding *individual throughput* to rewarding *system health*. Incentive pay should be tied directly to metrics from the leadership rewire dashboard (Chapter 9)—metrics like *decision cycle time*, *systemic autopsy rate (SAR)*, and *escalation quality*. This is how the CHRO makes *the 90-Day Leadership Rewire* a financial priority.

2. Incentivizing Delegation and Coaching

The most difficult behavioral change for leaders is moving from *doing* to *designing*.

- **The Rewire:** A significant portion of senior leader bonuses must be tied to the successful delegation rate and the talent mobility rate (TMR) of their direct reports. If a senior leader is compensated for their team's ability to operate autonomously (delegation rate) and successfully move into higher-judgment roles (TMR), they are financially incentivized to champion the rewire, not resist it.

THE CHRO AND THE EMERGING WORKFORCE

The structural and cultural changes driven by the CHRO are not just about maximizing AI leverage; they are essential for attracting and retaining the next generation of talent.

As we will explore in Chapter 14, the emerging workforce, specifically Gen Z, demands clarity, purpose, and impact. They intuitively distrust bureaucracy and demand the exact system the CHRO is now tasked with building:

- **Demand for Clarity:** They require clear guardrails, which the CHRO defines through job and competency architecture.
- **Demand for Impact:** They want to apply judgment, which the CHRO facilitates by eliminating low-value execution tasks (the Judgment Audit).
- **Distrust of Hierarchy:** They thrive in the fluid, modular structures the CHRO must now design.

By taking the lead on organizational transformation, the CHRO is proactively solving the talent crisis before it cripples the organization in Industry 5.0. The CHRO is the ultimate leader of the necessary people transformation, embedding agentic AI deeply into the talent, structure, and reward systems of the organization.

THE CHRO REWIRING TOOLKIT: A CHECKLIST FOR TRANSFORMATION

The transformation required by Industry 5.0 requires the CHRO to treat the organization as a living, adaptable system. This toolkit provides a practical checklist for the CHRO to use as the chief change agent and architect of the AI-ready organization, mapping actions directly to the three core functional areas of HR.

Pillar I: Rewiring Talent (Skills & Judgment)

Action	Diagnostic Question (What to Audit)	Alignment to HR Function
1. The Judgment Audit	Have we definitively mapped all high-volume, low-judgment tasks for agentic augmentation, isolating the 10 percent of tasks that require elevated human judgment?	**Talent Management** (Job Design/ Competency Mapping)
2. Prioritize Unlearning	Is there an explicit unlearning budget and mandated time for high-value employees to deliberately *stop* performing obsolete work and train on meta-cognition?	**Talent Management** (Learning & Development)
3. Build Agent Literacy	Is an advanced AI literacy program in place for *all* employees, focusing on prompt engineering, bias mitigation, and responsible AI usage (not just technical skills)?	**Talent Management** (Training/ Change Management)

Pillar II: Rewiring Structure (Fluidity & Design)

Action	Diagnostic Question (What to Audit)	Alignment to HR Function
4. Deconstruct Job Titles	Have we moved from rigid functional job titles to flexible *capability clusters* that allow talent to be deployed dynamically across agent-augmented workflows?	**Organizational Effectiveness** (Org Structure/Job Architecture)
5. Design for Modularity	Are our organizational design choices (e.g., federated or modular teams) eliminating unnecessary management layers and friction points created by old silos?	**Organizational Effectiveness** (Workforce Planning/ Efficiency)
6. Enforce Cultural Guardrails	Are the *systemic autopsy* and *candor* rules (Chapter 12) embedded in mandatory leadership training and consistently audited by the executive team?	**Organizational Effectiveness** (Culture/ Change Management)

Pillar III: Rewiring Incentives (Compensation & Accountability)

Action	Diagnostic Question (What to Audit)	Alignment to HR Function
7. Reward System Health	Are incentive and compensation schemes tied primarily to metrics of System Health (e.g., Decision Cycle Time, SAR) rather than individual output volume?	**Performance Management** (Incentives/ Goal Setting)
8. Incentivize Delegation	Is a portion of senior leader bonuses explicitly linked to their team's *delegation rate* and the Talent Mobility Rate (TMR) of their direct reports?	**Performance Management** (Leadership Assessment/ Coaching)
9. Secure the Future Pipeline	Are we actively redesigning the early career pipeline and training programs to attract the emerging workforce (Gen Z) by demonstrating organizational trust and high-impact judgment roles?	**Talent Management** (Recruitment/ Succession Planning)

The answers to these nine questions will serve as the CHRO's quarterly report card on organizational fitness, ensuring the long-term success of *the 90-Day Leadership Rewire.*

Chapter 14

The New Workforce Paradigm: Leading Generation Z in the Agentic Era

THE STRUCTURAL TRANSFORMATION championed by the CHRO is not merely a proactive defensive measure against technological disruption; it is the *mandatory response* to the demands of the emerging workforce.

Industry 5.0 is being led by machines, but it is being defined by the generations that grew up navigating constant technological change specifically Generation Z (born roughly 1997–2012).

This generation is the first cohort to enter the workforce with the complete ubiquity of decentralized technology and the simultaneous rise of powerful, consumer-facing AI. Their expectations, often labeled as "demands" by older generations, are in fact the precise *cultural prerequisites* for success in an agentic AI world. They are the ideal partners for the *Rewired* organization, but only if the organization is willing to shed its outdated assumptions about work.

THE GENERATIONAL CONTEXT OF DECENTRALIZATION

To understand Gen Z, we must understand the continuum of digital experience that shaped the talent pipeline.

Generation Y (Millennials) grew up during the rise of the internet and mobile phones (Shifts 1 & 2). Their defining organizational demands were *flexibility* (work/life balance) and *meaning* (purpose-driven roles). They are the pioneers of the knowledge economy, often translating analog leadership models into digital interfaces.

Generation Z (The Agentic Generation) grew up *inside* social media and mobile phone ubiquity. They are the first to encounter the consequences of decentralized technology information overload, digital authenticity crises, and algorithmic bias. Their demands center on *clarity* and *authentic impact*.

Generation Alpha, currently entering elementary and middle school, is the first truly AI-native generation, growing up with personalized, generative algorithms embedded in education, social life, and entertainment. Their future demand will be for *hyper-fluidity* the seamless, personalized integration of machine support into every task.

The immediate imperative for the *Rewired* leader is understanding and integrating Gen Z, the generation currently occupying critical entry and mid-level roles that will serve as the engine room for agentic adoption.

THE GEN Z MANDATE: CLARITY, PURPOSE, AND JUDGMENT

Gen Z's core traits are perfectly aligned with the needs of the agentic AI era, provided the organization meets them halfway.

1. The Demand for Clarity (The Guardrail Requirement)

Gen Z inherently rejects bureaucratic ambiguity, organizational opacity, and the "pay your dues" culture. Traditional leadership often prefers *intentional ambiguity* giving generalized direction without clear boundaries to test an employee's initiative. However, Gen Z sees ambiguity as *unnecessary friction* and evidence of poor leadership design. If the organization asks them to use judgment without clear boundaries, they will freeze up, not step up.

The *Rewired* solution is to provide the guardrails (Chapter 6) that *Rewired* leadership is designed to provide. Gen Z wants to know the boundaries of the decision-making sandbox so they can maximize the speed and quality of their judgment *within* those safe parameters. They do not need control; they need *contextual clarity*.

2. The Demand for Authentic Impact (The Systemic Accountability Requirement)

Gen Z is less tolerant of wasteful, low-value work. They demand that their work contribute to a verifiable, transparent purpose. They have a zero-tolerance policy for being treated as a *human router* for administrative friction. They will delegate, augment, or demand the elimination of work that can be done better or faster by an agent.

The *Rewired* solution involves leveraging the judgment audit (Chapter 13). By eliminating low-value execution and isolating high-judgment tasks, the organization immediately grants Gen Z the *impact* they seek. They do not want to work longer; they want their limited time to be spent on applied, high-leverage judgment.

3. The Skepticism of Authority (The Unlearning Requirement)

Gen Z's life experience has been curated by algorithms and often riddled with misinformation. This makes them highly sensitive to inauthenticity and hyper-aware of biases. Older leaders often rely on the *ego of expertise* (Chapter 10) and positional authority to drive decisions. The Gen Z response is to challenge the *source* and *logic* of decisions, not out of disrespect, but out of a learned skepticism.

This skepticism is a powerful asset for *adaptive intelligence* and the *90-Day Leadership Rewire* (Chapter 9). They are the perfect agents for *double-loop learning*, constantly asking, "Why is the system designed this way?" The *Rewired* leader treats Gen Z's skepticism as free, necessary system feedback.

LEADERSHIP EXAMPLE: THE CASE OF "QUIET DELEGATION"

To illustrate the critical failure of the old model, consider the experience of a major digital media company I advised recently. Their senior leadership was committed to "empowerment" but continued to use "quiet delegation" assigning tasks without providing the full context or the actual guardrails, assuming the Gen Z employees would "figure it out."

The result was a project failure. The Gen Z team didn't move forward because they lacked the specific clarity needed to *trust* their decentralized judgment. They simply *froze* in the ambiguous space, paralyzed by the fear of wasting organizational resources on an unvalidated path.

The failure wasn't a lack of initiative; it was a lack of *cultural safety* provided by the leaders. When the CEO finally stepped in, the question wasn't, "Why did you wait?" but *"Why did we fail to provide the guardrails that would make it safe for you to move?"* This shift from blaming the talent for inertia to blaming the system for ambiguity is the essence of *Rewired* leadership.

MY COACHING INSIGHTS: THE GEN Z MANDATE FOR CHANGE

While *Rewired* leaders must create the organizational environment, I have observed in my coaching work with *dozens of Gen Z employees and leaders* that they also have their own unlearning mandate. They must adapt their digital-native instincts to the realities of the agentic AI revolution.

Gen Z cannot simply wait for the organization to rewire; they must proactively master three core adaptive skills to survive Industry 5.0.

1. Unlearn: The Obsession with the "Perfect Answer"

Gen Z is adept at rapidly synthesizing information, but this often leads to a desire for a single, comprehensive, and perfect answer before action is taken.

The rewire for Gen Z is that they must unlearn the digital habit of information saturation and embrace *iterative judgment*. In the agentic era, the speed of iteration is more valuable than the perfection of the first draft. They must be comfortable acting with 70 percent information, trusting the system's ability to correct them quickly and safely.

2. Master: The Skill of Contextual Inquiry (The Prompt Power)

Gen Z is adept at searching, but the agentic AI revolution demands a higher level of questioning: *contextual inquiry*. This is the ability to ask the complex, non-linear questions that set the optimal guardrails for the agent.

The rewire for Gen Z involves mastering prompt crafting for strategic, high-stakes decisions. This means understanding not just *what* they want the agent to do, but *why* they are asking, and what ethical/organizational guardrails the agent must operate under. This elevates their role from user to "strategic agent-human integrator."

3. Unlearn: The Reliance on Digital Proxies

Gen Z is the most digitally social generation, but they often rely on digital proxies (slack, email, texts) for high-stakes, ambiguous conversations. This low-bandwidth communication is excellent for clear execution but fatal for navigating ambiguity.

The rewire for Gen Z requires unlearning the reluctance to engage in high-bandwidth ambiguity dialogue. When the problem is complex, when the guardrail is stressed, or when human judgment is truly required, they must default to face-to-face (physical or virtual) dialogue. Judgment is built in the complexity of real-time human interaction, not in asynchronous text. I constantly coach Gen Z leaders to move the most ambiguous 10 percent of their problems off-screen.

THE NEW SOCIAL CONTRACT: GEN Z AS CO-CREATORS

The structural changes demanded by the agentic AI era—fluid structures, focus on judgment, and systemic accountability—are exactly what Gen Z requires to thrive. The *Rewired* organization creates a new social contract with this talent pipeline: the partnership is based on *high-leverage impact,* not simply time served.

The CHRO's Role: Securing the Future Pipeline

The CHRO's playbook is directly validated by the Gen Z mandate. The CHRO must utilize Gen Z's demands as the internal catalyst for change:

1. **Weaponize the Skepticism:** Deploy Gen Z talent into "red team" roles focused on auditing and stress-testing the new guardrails and the performance of agentic systems. Their natural skepticism becomes a powerful risk mitigation tool.

2. **Make the Rewire Public:** When recruiting Gen Z, the organization must explicitly market its commitment to *systemic accountability* and the elimination of low-value work. The promise should not be just a job, but a high-impact role in a *safe, self-correcting system*.

3. **Invest in Agent Literacy as a Core Skill:** Gen Z requires training not just on *using* AI tools, but on the ethical and meta-cognitive challenges of collaborating with agents. This elevates their role from user to *agent-human integrator*.

THE FUTURE BEYOND Z: PREPARING FOR GEN ALPHA

While Gen Z is the immediate focus, the *Rewired* leader must also look ahead to Generation Alpha. This generation, raised with seamless AI assistance, will expect hyper-personalized work experiences and absolute fluidity between the physical and digital realms. The *90-Day Leadership Rewire* (Chapter 9) is the only process that will prepare the organization for the accelerating expectations of Gen Alpha. Continuous self-correction is the only way to avoid rapid obsolescence when the next talent generation arrives.

The *Rewired* leader recognizes that leading the new workforce paradigm is not about managing preferences; it is about embracing the structural changes required to survive Industry 5.0. Gen Z is not the problem; they are the catalyst and the solution, demanding the precise clarity and high-leverage judgment that the agentic era requires.

THE COACHING MANDATE FOR EMERGING LEADERS

My decades of coaching have proven that success in the agentic AI era is a function of unlearning outdated human habits and mastering new forms of cognitive rigor. For Gen Z and the rising Gen Alpha, this transition is the defining challenge of their professional lives. The goal of my coaching is not just to get them hired, but to equip them to *lead* this paradigm shift.

Coaching Mandate for Gen Z (The Adapters)

- **Mastering the 70 Percent Rule:** The primary lesson is that the value of an action is in its speed and its ability to gather feedback, not its initial perfection. I coach them to submit the 70 percent complete solution to the agent or the team, thereby accelerating the learning loop and avoiding the paralysis of perfectionism.
- **The Power of the 'Why':** I demand they preface every high-stakes agentic prompt with the organizational *context* and the ethical *why*. This forces them to think systemically, elevating them from prompt engineer to ethical decision architect.
- **Embracing Failure as Data:** I coach them to publicize their systemic failures, using the adaptive correction index (ACI) methodology. They become

the champions who convert organizational mistakes into shared, usable system data, accelerating the collective intelligence of the organization.

Coaching Mandate for Gen Alpha (The Integrators)

- **Human-First Judgment:** Since Gen Alpha will be accustomed to machine efficiency, I coach them to aggressively prioritize and defend the *human* necessity of their judgment. Their role will be to define the ethical boundaries that the machines cannot cross.
- **The Skill of Disintegration:** I coach them on the deliberate act of *separating* themselves from the continuous flow of AI assistance to practice pure, augmented, strategic thought. The greatest skill will be knowing when to turn the machine *off* to prevent cognitive atrophy.
- **Architectural Accountability:** Their focus must be on *designing* workflows and setting parameters, not executing them. They must see themselves not as workers, but as architects of the systems in which the machines operate.

The future of organizational success rests on the capacity of these emerging leaders to not only adapt to AI, but to actively define its parameters. My coaching ensures they are the architects, not the artifacts, of this revolution.

THE MARK ZIDES (#PACE) STANDARD OF EXCELLENCE SCORECARD: THE GEN Z READINESS INDEX

This scorecard provides the definitive, high-level metrics that *Rewired* leaders must continuously drive toward. Based on my work advising executive teams, these four KPIs are the gold standard for organizational fitness in the agentic AI revolution, confirming successful integration of the emerging workforce with the system redesign.

Strategic Outcome	Metric (Golden Standard KPI)	Target / Standard of Excellence	Rationale (The Strategic Why)
1. Systemic Risk Mitigation	Adaptive Correction Index (ACI)	> 95 percent	**Measures Trust & Learning:** A high ACI confirms the culture treats every error as a system design flaw, not a personnel failure. This mitigates risk by forcing continuous *adaptive correction*, validating the organizational commitment to growth.
2. Decision Velocity	Delegated Decision Cycle Time (DDCT)	< 48 Hours for 90 percent of delegated decisions.	**Measures Efficiency & Clarity:** Tracks the speed of decentralized action. Hitting this target confirms guardrails are clear and leaders have successfully unlearned the habit of bottlenecking.
3. Talent/ Adaptive Capacity	Talent Mobility Rate (TMR)	> 25 percent of high-potential talent transition capability clusters annually.	**Measures Fluidity & Engagement:** Confirms the organizational structure is dynamic, eliminating rigid job roles and offering the high-impact career growth Gen Z demands.
4. Leadership Fitness	Delegation Success Rate (DSR)	> 98 percent	**Measures Leader Behavior:** Tracks the percentage of delegated decisions that are *not* informally overridden or pulled back by senior leaders. This is the direct measure of the CEO's and executive team's *unlearning* success.

Chapter 15

The Unbearable Weight of Knowledge: Why Leaders Must Unlearn Their Own Success

EVERY LEADERSHIP TRANSFORMATION eventually comes to this moment.

Not a framework.

Not a system.

Not a strategy.

The moment when the leader realizes that the hardest work is not rewiring the organization. It is rewiring themselves.

This chapter is about that shift. Because no matter how elegant the operating model or how advanced the technology, leadership does not scale past the inner limits of the leader. When we speak of Industry 5.0, we speak of machines and systems, but ultimately, the true test lies in the single, most difficult act of human leadership: *letting go.*

THE LEADERSHIP MOMENT NO ONE TALKS ABOUT

I have seen this moment many times, usually behind closed doors.

It often happens late in the evening, after the meetings are done and the noise has quieted. A senior leader looks at their calendar for the next day and feels something unexpected.

Not pride.

Not urgency.

But weight.

Every decision routes through them. Every exception lands on their desk. Every risk feels personal. From the outside, they look indispensable. From the inside, they feel exhausted. One CEO said it to me plainly: "I built a company that can't move without me. And now I'm the problem."

That realization was not a failure. It was the beginning of rewiring.

THE COGNITIVE TRAPS: WHY SUCCESS BECOMES CONSTRAINT

Why does this weight accumulate? Because the very behaviors that earned leaders their position in the twentieth-century knowledge economy—the ability to be the quickest, the most decisive, and the most informed—have now created *systemic cognitive traps* that choke velocity in the agentic era.

1. The Indispensability Trap

The ego thrives on being the final stop. When leaders constantly solve every complex problem, they train the organization to stop learning, relying instead on the leader's eventual intervention. They build a company that is structurally dependent on their presence. In the agentic era, this dependency makes the entire system slower than the slowest human in the room: the leader. This trap directly reduces the delegation success rate (DSR).

2. The Certainty Tax

The traditional leader's power came from having the most complete, highest-resolution picture of reality. They demanded certainty before action. Today, agentic AI processes data in milliseconds and operates in perpetual beta. The leader who demands 100 percent certainty before acting imposes a *certainty tax* on the organization, sacrificing speed for outdated comfort. The cost of this tax is measured directly in the slow delegated decision cycle time (DDCT).

3. The Availability Bias

A leader's responsiveness—always answering the call, always jumping into the email thread—is a deep, ingrained habit. This *availability bias* trains teams that the quickest route to resolution is escalation, not personal judgment. As I observed with one senior executive: "I didn't realize how much my availability was training people to depend on me." The leader must stop being the solution to every problem and become the "architect of flow."

WHY THE LEADER MUST CHANGE FIRST

Organizations do not resist change. People resist uncertainty.

When leaders change how they lead, teams feel it immediately. When leaders say the right things but behave the same way, organizations stall. This is why rewiring the leader comes before rewiring culture. Leaders set the ceiling.

If a leader struggles to let go of control, the organization will never fully trust autonomy. If a leader steps in at the first sign of discomfort, teams will never develop judgment. If a leader avoids difficult conversations, clarity will always be fragile.

Rewired leadership begins internally.

THE HUMAN SKILLS THAT MATTER MORE THAN EVER

As AI and automation accelerate execution, human skills become the true differentiator of leadership. These are not soft skills; they are essential skills that must be aggressively developed.

Judgment

In a world of abundant data, judgment is the ability to decide when information is sufficient and action is required. *Rewired* leaders stop waiting for perfect answers. They decide within clear boundaries and move. *Judgment replaces certainty.*

Restraint

Restraint is the discipline to not step in too early. This is one of the hardest skills for experienced leaders because stepping in is what made them successful. *Rewired* leaders learn to sit with discomfort. They allow teams to struggle briefly within guardrails. They resist the urge to rescue. *Restraint creates learning. Learning creates scale.*

Trust

Trust is not blind faith. It is confidence built through clarity. *Rewired* leaders trust teams because decision rights are explicit, guardrails are clear, and accountability is real. Trust without clarity is chaos. *Clarity enables trust.*

Presence

Presence is not availability. It is intentional engagement where judgment matters most. *Rewired* leaders are present for: *ambiguity, conflict, trade-offs, and moments of consequence.* They are absent from routine execution. *Presence becomes leverage.*

Grit and Perseverance

Rewiring is uncomfortable. There will be moments when outcomes are imperfect, when decisions do not land cleanly, and when pressure tempts leaders to revert. *Rewired* leaders persist. They do not confuse temporary messiness with failure. They hold the line long enough for new behaviors to take root. That perseverance separates leaders who change systems from those who simply announce change.

THE INNER WORK OF REWIRED LEADERSHIP

Rewiring the leader is not about becoming distant or disengaged. It is about becoming intentional.

Rewired leaders develop new reflexes: pausing instead of reacting, asking instead of solving, and designing instead of controlling.

These reflexes take practice. They also require humility. The willingness to admit that what worked before may not work now is a sign of strength, not weakness.

A REAL LEADERSHIP SHIFT IN PRACTICE

I worked with a senior executive who prided himself on responsiveness. He answered everything. He reviewed everything. He was always available. He was also exhausted.

When he began rewiring, he did one thing first. He stopped responding immediately.

Instead, he asked one question consistently: *"Who owns this decision?"*

At first, it felt uncomfortable. People hesitated. Some mistakes were made.

Within weeks, something shifted. Teams stopped escalating prematurely. Decisions improved. The leader regained time and focus.

That is what rewiring looks like in practice. It is a slow, steady removal of the self from the operational loop, proving to the organization that the system is stronger than the individual.

THE LEADER'S REWIRE CHECKLIST

This checklist is not theoretical. It is practical. Leaders who rewire consistently do these things.

Timeframe	Action
Daily	Pause before stepping into decisions; Ask whether clarity or control is needed; Redirect ownership back to decision makers.
Weekly	Review where your time went; Identify one place you intervened unnecessarily; Reinforce one example of good judgment publicly.
Monthly	Audit decisions that escalated to you; Clarify or adjust guardrails where needed; Ask your team where leadership is slowing them down.
Quarterly	Reflect on where old habits are resurfacing; Revisit your leadership role and focus; Recommit to restraint, clarity, and trust.

Chapter 16
Unlearning the Leadership Ego

WE HAVE SPENT THE LAST SEVERAL CHAPTERS designing the system—clear guardrails, fluid structures, continuous adaptive correction. But the greatest, final resistance to the entire *90-Day Leadership Rewire* comes not from external forces, nor from technology, but from *the leader's own mind.*

The leadership ego is the internal, invisible force that resists decentralization. It is the deep, human need for validation that causes the leader to unconsciously insert themselves back into the decision flow, slowing the system and destroying the trust they worked ninety days to build.

In the agentic AI era, the ego is not just a personal weakness; it is the *single largest source of organizational friction* and the ultimate bottleneck to achieving the gold standard metrics we outlined.

THE EGO AS SYSTEMIC DRAG

Recall the delegation success rate (DSR) from the Mark Zides Standard of Excellence Scorecard. The DSR tracks the percentage of delegated decisions that are *not* informally pulled back or overridden. A low DSR is almost never a failure of process; it is a failure of *ego management.*

The ego fears decentralization because the leader's identity has historically been tied to *input* (being the one who knows the answer, works the longest, or signs the final document). When an agent or a junior team can perform the task faster and better, the ego experiences an identity crisis. The resulting defense mechanisms manifest as organizational drag:

- **The Unnecessary Question:** "Can you just walk me through the background again?" (A demand for validation disguised as due diligence.)
- **The Informal Veto:** "I trust your team, but on this one exception, I'll take it." (Undermining the guardrail for a momentary sense of control.)
- **The Hero Complex:** Waiting for a problem to escalate to the executive level so the leader can step in and "save the day."

This psychological friction is fatal to the speed of Industry 5.0. The leader must now unlearn the core assumptions of their own personal success.

THE THREE MANIFESTATIONS OF LEADERSHIP EGO

The leadership ego typically sabotages *the 90-Day Leadership Rewire* through three distinct, measurable vectors:

1. The Ego of Expertise (The Need to Be Right)

This is the belief that the leader's experience and their *history* give them superior foresight or knowledge compared to the agent-augmented team.

- **Sabotage:** This leader resists data that conflicts with their intuition, often dismissing the agent's recommendations or the decentralized team's judgment by saying, "I've seen this before."

- **The Counter-Measure:** The leader must actively champion the *question* over the *answer*. They must consciously shift their role from providing the solution to *diagnosing the systemic fault line* that the team is grappling with. Their expertise must be channeled into designing better guardrails, not overriding the current ones.

2. The Ego of Effort (The Need to Be Busy)

This is the psychological addiction to busyness, often tied to a belief that value is proportional to hours spent and decisions reviewed.

- **Sabotage:** This leader fills the vacuum created by delegation with low-value, high-visibility administrative work. They schedule unnecessary meetings, demand verbose reports, or fail to delete obsolete tasks, thereby modeling exactly the wrong behavior for the organization (the anti-leadership leverage equation).
- **The Counter-Measure:** The leader must embrace the *subtractive discipline.* Their performance review must be based on how much complexity and how many low-value tasks they have *removed* from the organization. True value is now measured by *design elegance*, not personal throughput.

3. The Ego of Certainty (The Fear of Being Blamed)

This is the most insidious ego function: the leader's fear that if a decentralized decision fails, the blame will ultimately land on their desk. This fear translates into a refusal to fully trust the system.

- **Sabotage:** This leader maintains parallel oversight systems—demanding copies of reports, asking for shadow briefings, or requiring pre-approval on matters technically delegated. This sends a loud, clear cultural message: "I don't trust the system I designed." This immediately reduces *psychological safety* and drops the DSR.

- **The Counter-Measure:** The leader must publicly commit to the adaptive correction index (ACI). By publicly stating that all failures are system failures *requiring adaptive correction*, they shield the team and focus accountability on the guardrails, not the individuals. The leader assumes full accountability for the system's *design*, thereby enabling the team's judgment.

THE INTERVENTION: THE "COAT CHECK OF COMMAND"

To help leaders consciously separate their personal ego from their systemic role, I often introduce a simple, fun, and memorable intervention: "The Coat Check of Command."

I worked with the executive team of a large manufacturing firm struggling with a consistently low DSR. The CEO, "Robert," was notoriously obsessed with being the smartest person in the room. He often dominated team strategy meetings with long-winded anecdotes about his past successes, overriding data and paralyzing decision-makers.

The solution was a light-hearted, ritualized intervention: During the next executive retreat focused on system performance, I introduced a large, velvet-rope stanchion and a brass coat rack at the entrance to the conference room. I handed Robert a large, ridiculous, novelty paper crown and a heavy satin cape.

I instructed him: "Robert, before you enter this room, you must check your command presence and your ego of expertise here. Until the meeting is over, you are no longer the CEO; you are the chief system architect. Your role is not to speak, but to ask questions about the quality of the system."

Robert, being a good sport, hung up the cape (the "ego of command") and the crown (the "ego of expertise") and hung up his actual jacket—which became the symbolic "coat check of command."

The power of the ritual was immediate and sustained:

- **Visual Reminder:** Whenever Robert started to dominate the discussion or revert to an anecdote, a designated team member would simply point to the empty coat rack.
- **Cultural Signal:** This public, ritualized act made it safe for the *entire team* to call out ego-driven behavior without career risk. It provided a shared language for stopping friction.
- **Role Clarity:** For the entire meeting, Robert defaulted to asking questions like, "Which guardrail should have handled that?" instead of "Why didn't you think of that?"

The coat check of command is a powerful metaphor: the leader must consciously and publicly shed the old definition of their value before entering any decision-making arena. Leadership in the agentic era requires constant, playful, and public self-correction.

THE ANTIDOTE: THREE DISCIPLINES OF EGO-LESS LEADERSHIP

To maintain the ego-less state necessary for a high DSR and high TMR, the *Rewired* leader must adopt three continuous disciplines:

1. Practice the 100 Percent to 0 Percent Shift

The leader must train themselves to go from 100 percent involvement in design (setting the guardrails, building the system) to *0 percent involvement in execution* (making the final operating decision). This binary approach prevents the insidious 15 percent involvement creep that causes systemic drift (Chapter 11). If the team is operating within the guardrail, the leader must commit to silence.

2. Seek Negative Feedback (The Inverse Validation)

The leader's ego thrives on praise. The antidote is to seek out data that challenges their self-perception. The leader should institutionalize "inverse validation"—asking for feedback not on their successes, but on where their presence or action *slowed the system*. "Tell me which decision I delayed this week, and why." This channels the leader's need for attention into systemic improvement.

3. Define Value by the System's Autonomy

The leader must redefine their personal value proposition. Their legacy is no longer the projects they championed, but the *quality and durability of the systems they designed.* A truly successful leader in Industry 5.0 is one whose organization continues to thrive, adapt, and correct itself perfectly even while the leader is on sabbatical. Their highest achievement is *organizational independence.*

Unlearning the leadership ego is the final and most personal act of the *90-Day Leadership Rewire*. It is the necessary sacrifice of personal vanity for the sake of organizational velocity. Only when the leader steps fully back can the decentralized power of agentic AI and the judgment of the emerging workforce step fully forward.

Chapter 17

The Red Flag Rule: The Systemic Mandate to Make Failure Safe

THE PRECEDING SIXTEEN CHAPTERS established that the greatest risk to a *Rewired* organization is not the agent's failure, but the *human's fear* of reporting it. The solution to this is to engineer a culture where truth and candor are rewarded ten times more than personal perfection.

This chapter introduces the structural mechanism that codifies this cultural shift: "The Red Flag Rule."

Psychological safety is often dismissed as a "soft" HR concept, but for the *Rewired* leader, it is the *hardest, most non-negotiable guardrail* to construct. It is the organizational infrastructure that determines whether your teams feel safe enough to use the judgment you've decentralized to them. If the culture rewards silence over candor, agentic AI will fail, not because the technology is flawed, but because the *human collaboration layer* is paralyzed by the fear of being wrong.

The adaptive correction imperative requires making failure safe. If teams are afraid of punishment, they will hide errors, stall decision-making, and hoard information. This is systemic friction, and it is a fatal threat to the speed required to survive Industry 5.0.

PSYCHOLOGICAL SAFETY AS AN ENGINEERING PROBLEM

Psychological safety is not about being nice; it is the *absence of interpersonal fear* that allows for productive dissent, risk-taking, and transparent error reporting. It is an engineering problem because you are deliberately designing the social environment to eliminate friction at critical behavioral points.

The ultimate measure of success for this imperative is the adaptive correction index (ACI). A high ACI > 95 percent confirms that every time a failure occurs, the default organizational response is to immediately diagnose the system, not blame the person. Low ACI means fear dominates.

The leader must engineer safety by identifying and eliminating three primary fear-friction points:

1. The Fear of Escalation (The Velocity Killer)

When an agent-augmented process encounters an ambiguous situation, a human must decide whether to act autonomously (risk correction) or escalate the decision. Fear causes the stall.

- **The Safety Mechanism:** The leader must redefine escalation as a *positive input*. Escalation is not failure; it is the *system working correctly*, signaling a guardrail is incomplete or a novel situation has been encountered. Leaders must publicly reward the fastest, most comprehensive escalation, proving that the speed of reporting is more important than the successful resolution.

2. The Fear of Candor (The Adaptive Killer)

Adaptive intelligence (Chapter 12) requires double-loop learning—questioning the assumptions behind the process.

This is impossible if people are afraid to criticize a senior leader's established strategy or the agent's recommendations.

- **The Safety Mechanism:** Leaders must institutionalize mechanisms like red teams or mandatory devil's advocacy where challenging the premise of a project is a *required* step, not a voluntary risk. This moves dissent from an act of insubordination to an act of organizational responsibility.

3. The Fear of Innovation (The Growth Killer)

The agentic AI revolution demands continuous experimentation, which means frequent failure. If failure leads to personal career penalties, experimentation stops.

- **The Safety Mechanism:** The leader must establish an explicit innovation failure budget. This budget funds designated pilots with the explicit expectation of a *high failure rate*. If the failure budget is not fully used, the leader should ask, "Why are we not failing enough?" This shifts the focus from avoiding mistakes to *maximizing learning velocity*.

THE STRUCTURAL SOLUTION: THE RED FLAG RULE

While the leader's emotional response is critical, the *Rewired* organization must also *engineer safety into its workflows*. The most powerful tool for this is the red flag rule.

The red flag rule is a structurally mandated requirement where specific high-risk, high-ambiguity points are built into a guardrail. When the decision-maker reaches this point, a red flag is automatically raised, and they are required to initiate a mandatory review huddle with predetermined experts or cross-functional leads before proceeding.

This system addresses the "fear of escalation" by making consultation a measure of *compliance and good judgment*, not a sign of personal failure.

Feature	The Red Flag Rule (Structural Safety)	Traditional Approval/ Veto Point (Ego Safety)
Goal	Improve the *quality* of the decision-maker's judgment by exposing it to challenge.	Offload **risk** and **accountability** to the senior approver/leader.
Outcome	The decision-maker remains the owner; the consultant shares perspective.	The approver assumes ownership; the decision-maker loses autonomy and learning opportunity.
Safety Impact	**High:** Raising the Flag is the required, safest path forward, eliminating the psychological burden of asking for help.	**Low:** Asking for approval is risky; if the decision fails, the team member is still often blamed.

Chapter 18

From Theory to Flow—Your 90-Day Implementation Manual

OOK, WE'VE SPENT SEVERAL CHAPTERS talking about the *system*, the *ego*, and the *guardrails*. That was the homework. Now, you're either in, or you're in the way.

This isn't a pilot program. This is the ninety-day uncorking. You have built a machine, and this manual is the ignition sequence. You don't get a pass because it's hard. You don't get a medal for announcing change. You get paid for *flow*—for eliminating every millisecond of friction between a business signal and an intelligent response.

The agentic AI revolution is a scale game run at speed. If you don't install the system, the system will install *your* obsolescence. Period.

The *Rewire* framework is the operating manual for the entire transformation—a structured, phased, ninety-day plan designed to install the new systems and behaviors required to achieve continuous organizational flow. This isn't about incremental gains; it's about exponential leverage.

THE TRIAD: GET YOUR ACT TOGETHER OR GET OUT

I've seen transformations die not from technical failure, but from *executive flinch*. The *Rewire* framework is ruthlessly cross-functional. It requires synchronized, non-negotiable leadership from the three executives who own the destiny of the modern organization. I call this the "Triad of Perpetuation."

Role	Core Rewire Mandate	The Non-Negotiable Hustle
CEO (The Architect)	Owns the vision and the delegation success rate (DSR).	**Model restraint.** Immediately shut down every informal override. You are the firewall against your own ego.
CHRO (The System Designer)	Owns the structure and the talent mobility rate (TMR).	**Kill the Job Description.** Execute the Judgment Audit to eliminate 40 percent of all low-value execution tasks by day sixty.
CTO/ CIO (The Flow Engineer)	Owns the agentic implementation and the delegated decision cycle time (DDCT).	**Decimate the Latency.** Ensure the system allows a decentralized decision to clear within forty-eight hours by day ninety.

This Triad must meet *daily for fifteen minutes* for the first ninety days. Not weekly. *Daily.* You are checking the metrics and forcing flow. No excuses.

PHASE 1: DIAGNOSIS AND THE UNFORGIVING AUDIT (DAYS 1 – 30)

This phase is about diagnosis. It's the uncomfortable truth-telling. You are finding the rot and cauterizing it. You are establishing the base camp for scale.

Command 1: The Vow of Systemic Accountability (Day 1)

The CEO stands up and declares the end of the "age of blame." The public statement must be uncompromising: *"All future failures are system failures. Period. We will use the* adaptive correction index (ACI) *to find the faulty guardrail, not the faulty human."* This single act establishes the red flag rule as the governing law of your culture. If you flinch here, you lose.

Command 2: The Judgment Audit (Days 2 – 15)

The CHRO and CTO run this joint operation. This is not HR busywork; this is the surgical removal of low-value friction. You are mapping 80 percent of all middle-manager tasks.

- **The 3-Bucket Test:** Every task must be ruthlessly sorted:
  - » Execution *(Delegate to Agent)*
  - » Coordination *(Delegate to System/Guardrail)*
  - » Judgment *(Keep for Human)*

- **The Target:** You must identify enough execution tasks to free up 25 percent of human time by the end of this phase. If you're not cutting deeply, you're not serious.

Command 3: The Guardrail Foundation (Days 16 – 30)

You don't need a thousand pages of policy. You need five, rock-solid guardrails that contain 80 percent of your financial and regulatory risk. The CEO owns the clarity.

- **Rule of Precision:** Each guardrail must define the:
  - » Decision Owner
  - » Accountability Metric

» Red Flag Rule Trigger (The non-negotiable stop point)

- **The Output:** A minimal viable guardrail set. If it's complex, it's broken. Keep it simple and focus the entire organization on mastering these five rules.

Command 4: Baseline the Zides Scorecard

Measure where you are right now. Your low DSR is the debt you owe your teams. Your slow DDCT is the cash you're leaving on the table. You can't manage what you don't measure. Get the numbers. No self-deception.

PHASE 2: BUILD, VALIDATE, AND FORCE THE FLOW (DAYS 31 – 60)

This is the high-tension build phase. You are actively dismantling old structures while new ones are still unstable. This requires nerve.

Command 5: The Agentic Integration Firestorm (Days 31 – 40)

The CTO pushes 100 percent of the low-value execution tasks identified in the audit to agents or automated systems. No phased rollouts. Hard cutover. If a team complains, the CEO supports the CTO. You are forcing the organization to find its new, high-leverage work.

- **The Mandate:** Every agent must have a clear defined by the ACI process. When the agent fails, the system learns.

Command 6: The Capability Cluster Launch (Days 41 – 50)

The CHRO launches the first true capability cluster (Chapter 13) in a critical business area. This cluster operates with full autonomy under the new guardrails. This is your proof of concept for structural fluidity.

- **No "Sacred Cows":** The old job titles and roles are dissolved in this cluster. Talent is rewarded for *versatility and judgment*. Track the TMR relentlessly. If talent isn't moving, the cluster is stagnating.

Command 7: The Red Flag Enforcement (Days 51 – 60)

This is the hinge point. The red flag rule is formally enforced across all new guardrails. The CEO must personally audit the first five red flags raised in the pilot cluster.

- **The 10X Response:** The CEO's response to the team that raises the first red flag even if it reveals a costly error must be ten times more positive than their internal panic. *You are validating the system of safety.* The leader who punishes the red flag is signing the company's death warrant.
- **The DSR Spike:** Watch your delegation success rate (DSR). If it starts to climb, it means the teams trust the safety net. If it drops, the leader's ego is interfering.

PHASE 3: SCALE, SUSTAIN, AND UNLEASH THE FORCE (DAYS 61 – 90)

The final push is about cementing the cultural shift and ensuring the system is self-correcting—that it is truly an unstoppable force.

Command 8: The ACI Takedown and Public Audit (Days 61 – 75)

The ACI is your new north star. The Triad conducts the first public audit of the ACI data. You are not celebrating successes; *you are celebrating intelligent failures.*

- **The Proof of Flow:** Select the most significant failure since day sixty. Publicly detail the guardrail that failed and the surgical correction made. Show the company that mistakes are the fuel for the adaptive correction index.
- **The Culture of Judgment:** The CHRO ties a portion of executive bonuses to ACI and DSR improvement—not revenue alone. You are paying for flow, not execution.

THE PROOF OF FLOW: THE TRINITY CAPITAL CASE STUDY

The true measure of the *Rewire* framework is the conversion of systemic risk into adaptive correction. To prove this, we look at Trinity Capital, a major multi-national financial services firm that was choking on its own success.

The Intervention: Enforcing the Red Flag Rule at High Stakes

Before the *Rewire*, Trinity's DDCT was twenty-two days, and their culture was paralyzed. The Triad launched the framework, focusing the red flag rule on a single, critical guardrail: *automated high-frequency trading policy updates.*

1. **The New Guardrail:** The policy update was automated but triggered a red flag rule if the potential liability exceeded $500,000. The rule required an immediate mandatory

review huddle with the legal and risk architects (a structural safety check).

2. **The Test of Fire (Day 78):** A new agentic model tripped the red flag, signaling a $650,000 liability risk under volatile market conditions. The trading desk manager was internally panicking, but the red flag rule removed the choice: compliance was mandatory.

3. **The CEO's 10X Response:** CEO Michael was immediately notified. He suppressed his internal panic and delivered the non-negotiable 10X rule response: *"The system worked exactly as designed. The red flag is an asset. [Manager's Name], you protected the firm. Your first priority is not the trade but documenting the architectural gap that allowed the risk to reach this level."*

4. **The ACI Audit:** The public audit determined that the agent had followed the *literal* command of the old guardrail, but the guardrail itself contained a flawed assumption about market volatility (a system error).

THE OUTCOME: FLOW STATE ACHIEVED

The Trinity Capital case study provided the necessary cultural shock. The organization realized that failure was not a career-ender, but a *system upgrade*.

Metric	Baseline (Pre-Rewire)	Day 90 Outcome	Impact / ROI
Delegated Decision Cycle Time (DDCT)	22 Days	4 Days	**82 percent Velocity Improvement.** Market opportunities were captured immediately.

Metric	Baseline (Pre-Rewire)	Day 90 Outcome	Impact / ROI
Adaptive Correction Index (ACI)	Near 0 percent	88 percent	**Cultural Shift:** Errors were reported 7x faster, turning latent risk into active learning.
Delegation Success Rate (DSR)	55 percent	93 percent	**Trust:** Leaders stopped intervening, trusting the guardrails and the red flag safety net.

The Trinity Capital transformation proves that the red flag rule and the 10X rule are the *high-leverage, structural tools* that unlock exponential velocity by making the organization safe enough to scale its own judgment.

Command 9: The Ego Audit and the DSR Mandate (Days 76 – 90)

The CEO and senior leadership run the Zides' Standard of Excellence Scorecard (Chapter 14) on themselves. This is uncomfortable, but mandatory.

- **Personal Accountability:** Leaders must publicly share their biggest personal failure in restraint (their highest-friction intervention). You must model the vulnerability you demand from your teams.
- **The DSR Mandate:** For every guardrail, the DSR must be above 85 percent. If a leader's DSR is low, they are failing the system. Their mandate is not to fix the team; it is to *fix their own behavior* and *the guardrail's clarity*.

Command 10: The Unstoppable Loop (Day 91 and Beyond)

You shift from a project mindset to a *perpetual operating rhythm*. The daily Triad meeting becomes the quarterly *Rewire* review, focused entirely on auditing the guardrail architecture against the ACI data.

- **The Final Goal:** The organization must
  be able to adapt to the next agentic AI
  technology the one you don't even know
  about yet without executive intervention.
  Your job is to make the system *out-adapt the
  competition and out-live the current leader.*

A FINAL THOUGHT

The *Rewire* framework is not about making people comfortable. It's about making your organization *uncomfortable with slowness, ambiguity, and control.*

You now have the map, the tools, the metrics, and the timeline.

Stop talking. *Execute.* The speed of agentic AI demands nothing less than absolute, uncompromising flow.

Chapter 19

The Architect of Flow: Designing Your Legacy by Mastering the Art of Letting Go

YOU HAVE BUILT THE MACHINE. YOU HAVE survived the ninety days. Now, you stand at the threshold of the most profound leadership challenge: Day 91.

Day 91 is the moment the adrenaline stops. The crisis is over. And you are left alone with a perfect, self-correcting system.

This is where of transformations fail. They fail because the leader, bored or anxious, reaches back in and breaks the system. They confuse *relevance* with *interference*. They believe their experience dictates intervention, even when their design dictates *restraint*.

This chapter is about preventing that relapse. It is the "last unlearning"—the acceptance that your greatest mark of leadership is not how well you run the company, but how well the company runs *without you*.

Your job is no longer to be the hero player; it is to be the architect of flow.

THE TRAP OF THE HERO EGO

The *hero ego* is your enemy now. It craves the urgent approval, the crisis fix, and the public moment of rescue. It demands the dopamine hit of being the smartest person in the room.

But in a *Rewired* organization:

- If you must *save the day*, your guardrails failed.
- If you must *make the final call*, your judgment architecture is weak.

The only way to move from player to architect is through "radical restraint."

Radical restraint is the ability to see a problem, know the answer, and *choose not to give it*, because giving the answer prevents the system from solving itself.

THE SILENT 48 RULE

Here is your most critical new daily habit: "The Silent 48."

When a metric dips, or a project hits a snag that doesn't trigger an automatic red flag, you must wait before asking a single question.

- **Why?** Because the system needs time to learn. If you intervene at hour two, you teach the team and the AI to stop thinking and just wait for the CEO. Your anxiety kills their autonomy.
- **The Reward:** By waiting, you usually receive a report stating: "Problem identified, guardrail updated, flow restored." Your silence becomes the sound of the system working.

THE NEW COGNITIVE DISCIPLINE: DON'T ASK FOR THE ANSWER, ASK FOR THE ARGUMENT

Here is the tactical reality that challenges every leader: The instant availability of tools like Gemini, ChatGPT, and Claude.

The question I get from every executive is: "If the AI can generate the perfect marketing strategy in ten seconds, shouldn't I just ask it for the answer?"

No. That is laziness. That is abdication.

If you ask an LLM, *"What should our Q3 strategy be?"* you are outsourcing your soul. You are asking for an average output based on the average of the internet. That is how you build a mediocre company at the speed of light.

The *Rewired* leader uses AI not as an oracle, but as an *assault weapon* against their own bias.

THE "PING" PROTOCOL: HOW TO LEAD WITH LLMS

When you interact with your agentic tool, your role is not the student; it is the "Supreme Court Justice." You are testing the limits of the proposed strategy.

Don't Ask for Solutions; Ask for Blind Spots.

- **The Flaw:** Asking for the solution yields the path of least resistance.
- **The Rewired Prompt:** "Here is *my* plan to launch this product. Act as our fiercest competitor. Tell me exactly why this plan will fail and list three regulatory risks I have ignored."
- **The Shift:** You use the AI to destroy your confirmation bias, not to confirm it. You force the agent to play the devil's advocate.

Don't Ask for Agreement; Ask for Conflicts.

- **The Flaw:** Human teams hide internal conflicts to present a unified front. The agent can find these conflicts instantly.
- **The Rewired Prompt:** "Read these four departmental reports. Tell me where marketing's assumptions about customer behavior *conflict* with finance's budget allocations."
- **The Shift:** You use AI to synthesize the contradictions, bringing the highest-leverage friction point—the guardrail gap—directly to your desk.

The Leader's Final Job: Defending the "Why."

The AI provides the 'what' (data) and the 'how' (execution steps). Your job is to provide the 'why'—the mission, the values, the long-term vision, and the emotional justification for the risk.

The Rule: The AI provides the 'how' and the 'what if.' *You* provide the 'why' and the final *judgment*. If you let the machine define your purpose, you are finished.

THE THREE ARCHETYPES OF PERPETUITY

If you aren't making every decision, you are pivoting your role to sustained leadership. Your job is to lead in three dedicated modes of existence:

The Boundary Steward (the CEO's New Job):

- **Mandate:** Protect the guardrails from being changed, bypassed, or over-complicated.

- **Practical Action:** You enforce the "deletion rule": For every new guardrail proposed, one old one must be retired. You fight for simplicity because complexity is the enemy of flow.

The Judgment Coach (the CHRO's New Job):

- **Mandate:** Develop the people who use the system, focusing on the quality of their judgment, not the outcome of their decision.
- **Practical Action:** You only coach on the guardrail gap. When a decision goes wrong, you ask: "Where did the guardrail fail to cover this situation?" This turns the failed person into an architect of the system.

The Ethical Architect (the CTO's New Job):

- **Mandate:** Ensure the agentic AI serves human values, not just pure efficiency.
- **Practical Action:** You monitor the productive tension between humans and machines. You ensure there is a clear, codified process for when human judgment must override an agent's recommendation, reinforcing the final authority of human values.

PRACTICAL LEADERSHIP EXAMPLES: SUSTAINING THE FLOW

The true test of *Rewired* leadership is when the money is on the line. These examples show how to lead with the system, not the ego.

1. The Compensation Shift: Rewarding the System, Not the Hero

- **The Scenario:** A manager bypassed protocol and personally saved a huge delivery after a system failure. The old culture would give him a $10,000 bonus.
- **The Rewired Action:** The CEO (boundary steward) publicly thanks the manager for their speed but gives the major system award (a grant or bonus) to the team that immediately documented the guardrail flaw that caused the failure.
- **The Principle:** You publicly reinforce: "We don't pay for heroes; we pay for systems. Our highest value is prevention, not rescue."

2. The Budget Override Test: Delegating the Financial Veto

- **The Scenario:** A high-level team, following their guardrail, requests a million dollar discretionary budget. The CFO feels the request is too risky and wants to use their traditional veto.
- **The Rewired Action:** The CEO enforces *restraint* on the CFO. The budget is approved because the guardrail was followed. The CFO's new job is to design the failure guardrail—a clear, automatic condition (e.g., if project returns drop below for sixty days) that *immediately triggers a mandatory ACI audit* and budget suspension.
- **The Principle:** Financial risk is managed by the system's design, not the executive's intuition. The power shifts from "no (control) to "when and how to stop (clarity).

3. The Data Hoarding Audit: Fighting Systemic Friction

- **The Scenario:** Audits show that three different departments are hoarding incompatible customer data, causing friction. When challenged, managers cite "data ownership."
- **The Rewired Action:** The CHRO (judgment coach) removes all "data ownership" policies. They mandate that ACI credit the internal cultural reward for fixing system flaws will only be granted if the correction utilizes a single, centralized data platform.
- **The Principle:** This uses the system's own reward mechanism to force data sharing, proving that the culture is built around *flow*, not territorial control.

THE FINAL CHARGE: LEADERSHIP THAT LASTS

You have spent a career accumulating power, authority, and control. The last unlearning asks you to give it back. It asks you to trade the shallow satisfaction of being the "hero" for the deep, enduring legacy of being the "architect."

If you can master the discipline of radical restraint and use AI to sharpen, not replace, your judgment, you won't just build a successful company. You will build an entity that creates value, grows leaders, and adapts to the future long after you have left the building.

You will have built something that matters. And that, in the end, is the only leadership metric that counts.

Conclusion

A Manifesto for the Rewired Leader: The Choice to Matter

THIS FINAL CHAPTER IS NOT A SUMMARY; IT IS a *manifesto*. It is the codification of the choice you must now make.

Every generation of leaders inherits a model of leadership.

They don't choose it.

They absorb it.

It comes from how they were managed, what was rewarded, and what worked at the time. And for a long time, that model served leaders well. It helped them scale teams, build companies, and deliver results in a world that moved at the speed of human communication.

But every leadership model eventually meets its limit. The world of work has changed faster than leadership habits. Technology now moves at machine speed. Agentic AI initiates work, surfaces decisions, and reshapes how value is created. Organizations no longer wait for permission. Markets no longer reward caution disguised as control.

And leadership, as it has traditionally been practiced, is being exposed. Not because leaders are incapable, but because the system they mastered no longer matches the world they are leading.

This book exists for leaders who recognize that truth and are willing to act on it.

THE BROKEN CONTRACT: WHY "GOOD" LEADERSHIP IS NOW A LIABILITY

For decades, leadership operated under an unspoken contract. Leaders were expected to know the answers and make the decisions. In return, organizations moved at a manageable pace. That contract is broken.

It is broken not because you failed, but because the environment changed. Work now happens continuously, not episodically. Yet, I see "linear leaders" everywhere operating as if the old contract applies. They insert themselves everywhere. They review constantly. They approve reflexively. And the organization slows down around them. In Industry 5.0, this behavior is not leadership.

You can keep leading the way that made you successful. You can work harder every year to maintain control. You can hire more middle managers to read the reports the AI generates. You can try to be the heroic gatekeeper of a world that has already overrun the gates. Or you can *rewire your leadership* and design for the world that already exists.

One path leads to exhaustion and diminishing impact. The other leads to leverage, relevance, and scale. There is no neutral option.

THE LINEAR LEADER VS. THE EXPONENTIAL LEADER

To understand the stakes, we must look at the two diverging paths of the modern executive.

The Linear Leader believes their value is additive. They believe that for the company to do more, *they* must do more.

They are the hardest working person in the room. They are also the ceiling. Because their organization can only move as fast as they can read an email, approve a request, or attend a meeting, their growth curve is flat. They are fighting a mathematical war they cannot win.

The Exponential Leader believes their value is multiplicative. They understand that for the company to do more, they must do *less*. They do not build dependency; they build capacity. By leading with *restraint* and trusting the ACI, they remove the ceiling. Their organization scales at the speed of the system, not the speed of the leader.

The choice is binary. You cannot be both.

WHAT REWIRED LEADERSHIP REALLY IS

Rewired Leadership is not about becoming hands-off. It is not about delegating everything. It is not about trusting blindly. ***Rewired Leadership* is about designing leadership so it scales.**

It is the shift from:

- **Control to Clarity:** Replacing the need to check work with the discipline of defining the guardrail.
- **Presence to Leverage:** Replacing the need to be in the meeting with the design of the system that runs the meeting.
- **Approval to Guardrails:** Replacing the veto power with the red flag rule.
- **Heroics to Systems:** Replacing the "save the day" mentality with the "fix the architecture" discipline.

Rewired leaders stop asking, "How do I stay involved?" They start asking, "How do I design this so I don't have to be?" This is not abdication. It is evolution.

LEADERSHIP IN AN AGENTIC WORLD: THE NEW PHYSICS OF WORK

Rewired leaders do not compete with machines. They design the environment in which machines and humans work together. They decide who owns decisions. They define where automation acts. They clarify where escalation matters.

There are a few hard truths few leaders want to confront:

- **Persistent slowness signals design failure.**
  (The problem is not your people.)
- **Team hesitation signals unclear authority.**
  (The problem is not your team's capability).
- **Underperforming AI signals structural mismatch.**
  (The problem in not your technology).

In an agentic world:

- **Unclear decision rights create chaos.**
  (The agent acts on bad instructions).
- **Excessive approvals create delay.** (The agent waits for a human who is asleep).
- **Inconsistent leadership behavior creates mistrust.** (The team hides the agent's failure).

Leadership that made sense in a slower era becomes a bottleneck in a faster one. What once felt responsible now feels restrictive. What once created safety now creates delay.

Rewired leaders have the courage to see this without defensiveness. They understand that relevance is not preserved by holding on. It is preserved by *letting go*.

This is leadership at a higher altitude. It is the role of the chief architect of flow.

THE PERSONAL RECKONING: THE THREE VOWS OF THE REWIRED LEADER

Every leader who finishes this book arrives at the same moment. A quiet reckoning. The realization that rewiring the organization is impossible without rewiring the leader. To bridge the gap between who you are and who you must become, you must commit to three non-negotiable vows. These are the practical, emotional, and behavioral anchors of your new reality.

Vow 1: The Vow of Radical Restraint (The Ego Check)

I vow to recognize that my experience may just be the obstacle in my way. When I believe I know the answer, I will remember every time I provide the answer, I am robbing the system of the ability to learn it.

When a problem arises and I feel the physical urge to intervene, I promise to pause. I will ask myself honestly: Is the system broken, or am I simply uncomfortable?

If the red flag rule is being followed, I will not step in. I will allow the ACI process to unfold as designed.

I will resist the instinct to control, even when silence feels painful.

I choose the discipline of trust over the ease of interference, and the long-term strength of the system over the short-term comfort of my authority.

Vow 2: The Vow of Psychological Safety (The Candor Check)

I vow to build systems where truth is not feared. I accept that a system fails when its people are conditioned to hide error instead of reveal it.

When failure, loss, or systemic weakness is brought to me, I promise to honor the messenger.

I commit to the 10X Rule: I will respond with ten times more grace, curiosity, and steadiness than my ego demands.

I will listen before I judge.

I will ask before I defend.

I will seek understanding before assigning blame.

I will reward honesty in public and protect it in private.

I will never punish the truth that strengthens the system.

I choose psychological safety over fragile pride, and enduring integrity over the illusion of control.

Vow 3: The Vow of Design Purity (The Simplicity Check)

I vow to recognize that growth naturally accumulates complexity. I will remember that addition is the default—and restraint is my responsibility.

I commit to being a relentless subtractor. I will follow the deletion rule: I will not add a new guardrail without removing an old one. I will not introduce a new metric without retiring one that no longer serves.

I will fight for the purity of flow in how work moves and decisions are made. I will treat bureaucracy not as safety, but as technical debt—something to be paid down deliberately, not allowed to compound.

I choose clarity over accumulation, simplicity over false protection, and disciplined removal as a core act of leadership.

The only question is whether leadership will move with it.

THE FINAL WORD

Rewired leadership is not a trend.

It is not a framework.

It is not optional.

It is the leadership model of this era.

Leaders who embrace it will scale organizations that move faster, learn quicker, and adapt continuously. They will build the "exponential firm"—an entity that grows in value and intelligence independently of the leader's hours worked.

Leaders who ignore it will slowly become the constraint they never intended to be. They will become the "linear leader" in an exponential world, wondering why their hard work no longer yields results.

The future of leadership does not belong to those who cling to control.

It belongs to those who design for flow.

It belongs to those who have the courage to trust the system they built.

It belongs to those who **Rewire.**

Go design something that lasts.

Thank you for reading!!
Mark Zides
CEO | Best-Selling Author

Appendix

THE 90-DAY LEADERSHIP REWIRE™ CHECKLIST

Days 1–30: Reset

- ☐ Stop rescuing decisions
- ☐ Observe AI-human friction
- ☐ Map escalation patterns
- ☐ Let discomfort surface

Days 31–60: Reframe

- ☐ Redesign decision rights
- ☐ Define AI and human guardrails
- ☐ Shift from outcome review to logic review
- ☐ Communicate intent relentlessly

Days 61–90: Reinforce

- ☐ Publicly reward judgment
- ☐ Defend autonomy under pressure
- ☐ Convert errors into guardrail upgrades
- ☐ Measure system health, not effort

THE LEADER'S PERSONAL REWIRE CHECKLIST

Daily

- ◻ Pause before intervening
- ◻ Ask: "Is this clarity or control?"
- ◻ Redirect ownership

Weekly

- ◻ Identify one unnecessary intervention
- ◻ Publicly reinforce good judgment

Monthly

- ◻ Audit escalations
- ◻ Tighten one guardrail

Quarterly

- ◻ Name one habit to unlearn
- ◻ Remove one source of friction

THE REWIRED LEADERSHIP™ OPERATING SYSTEM

Leadership is no longer defined by presence, authority, or expertise. In an AI-enabled organization, leadership is defined by system design.

The *Rewired Leadership™* Operating System is a practical framework for building organizations where humans and AI work together without slowing each other down and where judgment, trust, and accountability scale instead of bottleneck.

This operating system has five core components. When any one is weak, leadership friction increases. When all five are aligned, organizations move faster with less noise, fewer escalations, and stronger leaders at every level.

1. Clarity

Clarity defines why the system exists and what matters now. *Rewired* leaders eliminate ambiguity before they demand performance. They ensure that intent, priorities, and outcomes are understood without repeated explanation or escalation. In a clear system, people do not wait for permission—they act with confidence.

- **Signal of strength:** Teams can explain priorities without slides or approval.
- **Signal of failure:** Leaders are repeatedly asked to restate direction.

2. Decision Design

Decision Design defines how authority flows through the organization.

Instead of relying on hierarchy and approvals, *Rewired* leaders intentionally design decision rights. Ownership is explicit. Guardrails replace permissions. Escalation becomes the exception, not the default.

This is where leadership shifts from control to architecture.

- **Signal of strength:** Decisions move quickly at the edge of the organization.
- **Signal of failure:** Leaders become approval bottlenecks.

3. Judgment Allocation

Judgment Allocation defines who decides what—humans or AI.

In a *Rewired* system:

- AI handles execution, analysis, and coordination.
- Humans handle ambiguity, ethics, trade-offs, and meaning.

Leadership failure occurs when judgment is either hoarded at the top or abdicated to machines. Rewired leaders deliberately protect and elevate human judgment where it matters most.

- **Signal of strength:** Humans spend time on judgment, not busywork.
- **Signal of failure:** Leaders are buried in decisions AI could already support.

4. Trust Architecture

Trust Architecture defines how autonomy is earned and expanded.

Trust is not a personality trait—it is a designed system. *Rewired* leaders create environments where competence increases freedom, mistakes produce learning, and truth travels faster than fear.

Without trust, AI creates speed but not resilience. With trust, autonomy scales.

- **Signal of strength:** Teams surface issues early without fear.
- **Signal of failure:** Leaders only hear problems when they become crises.

5. Adaptive Correction

Adaptive Correction defines how the system learns.

Rewired organizations treat failure as feedback. Instead of blaming individuals, leaders upgrade guardrails, decision rights, and workflows. The system improves continuously - without disruption or heroics.

This is how leadership becomes durable, not reactive.

- **Signal of strength:** The organization gets faster over time.
- **Signal of failure:** The same problems repeat quarter after quarter.

Why This Matters

AI does not replace leaders. It exposes leadership systems that were already broken. The *Rewired Leadership*™ Operating System gives leaders a way to:

- Scale judgment
- Reduce friction
- Increase trust
- Move faster without losing control
- Lead effectively in a human + AI world

Leadership is no longer about being the smartest person in the room.

It's about designing a system where the room gets smarter every day.

Glossary of Acronyms

AAR	After Action Reviews
ACI	Adaptive Correction Index
ACR	Assumption Challenge Rate
CEO	Chief Executive Officer
CFO	Chief Financial Officer
CHRO	Chief Human Resources Officer
CLO	Chief Learning Officer
CTO	Chief Technology Officer
DDCT	Delegated Decision Cycle Time
DSR	Delegation Success Rate
EQ	Emotional Intelligence
HR	Human Resources
IP	Intellectual Property
IQ	Intelligence Quotient
KPI	Key Performance Indicator
M&A	Mergers and Acquisitions
MVE	Minimum Viable Experiences
MVP	Minimum Viable Products
P&L	Profit and Loss
SAR	Systemic Autopsy Rate
SMB	Small-to-Medium Business
TMR	Talent Mobility Rate
VP	Vice President

About the Author

MARK ZIDES IS A seasoned executive, founder, and leadership advisor with more than thirty-five years of experience helping organizations transform how work gets done at the intersection of HR, talent, leadership, and AI.

He is the bestselling author of *The #PACE Process for Early Career Success*, which helped a generation of Millennials and GenZ professionals build clarity and momentum early in their careers. His work has since evolved to focus on a broader challenge facing organizations today: how leaders and HR teams must redesign work, skills, and leadership models as AI reshapes the workforce.

Mark previously served as CEO and President of Luminoso Technologies, an AI-powered text analytics company that helps enterprises make sense of employee and customer feedback at scale. He partnered closely with senior CX leaders to turn human insight into smarter workforce decisions and more adaptive organizations.

Earlier, he founded and led CoreAxis Consulting, an award-winning learning and talent transformation firm that partnered with organizations including Amazon, Bank of

America, Thermo Fisher Scientific, and Netflix to deliver large-scale leadership development, workforce upskilling, and enterprise learning programs.

A TEDx speaker, Mark is known for challenging outdated models of management, learning, and performance. His work blends human-centered leadership with AI-enabled insights to help organizations reimagine work, develop future-ready talent, and lead through continuous change.

His point of view is clear: the future of work is not an HR initiative—it is a leadership imperative.

www.ingramcontent.com/pod-product-compliance
Lightning Source LLC
Chambersburg PA
CBHW070926130626
46555CB00001B/312